AGILE & SCRUM MADE SIMPLE

SIMPLE

NOTES FROM MY EXPERIENCE....

ANCY CHERIAN

XpressPublishing
An imprint of Notion Press

XpressPublishing
An Imprint of Notion Press

No.8, 3rd Cross Street,CIT Colony,
Mylapore, Chennai, Tamil Nadu-600004

ISBN 978-1-63714-108-3

To my parents who always believed in me and knew I could do it.

And my husband and my son for telling me I should give it a shot.

Contents

Contents

Preface

With more focus on continuous improvement, agile project management beats the traditional linear way of managing projects as well as developing products and services. Increasingly, many organizations are slowly adopting the agile project management methodology since it uses a series of some shorter product development cycles for great project success. This project management style allows for continuous integration, rapid development, and continuous delivery.

Agile is a project management methodology that breaks down larger projects into smaller, manageable chunks known as iterations. At the end of every iteration, something of value is produced. The product that's produced during every iteration should be able to be placed into the world to receive feedback from stakeholders or users.

Contrary to Waterfall project management, agile is strictly sequenced: you do not commence design until research is complete and development doesn't commence until all designs are signed off. With agile, developers, designers, and business people are simultaneously working together. With the agile methodology, there's a higher level of quality improvements on an incremental basis rather than waiting to distribute the finished projects. According to a PWC report, agile projects are 28% more successful than traditional methodologies.

This book is short and to the point which provides Agile knowledge for the ScrumMasters, Product Owners and Agile Software Developers: Backlog, User Stories, Sprint, Retrospectives.. It will be your steadfast companion if you are planning to adopt Agile. Whether you are just starting out or are already an advanced user, 'Agile & Scrum made Simple' will provide you with a 360-degree guide that covers every stage of the transition from getting started, helping individuals into new roles, structuring teams, scaling up, working with a distributed team, to implementing effective metrics and continuous improvement.The book focuses mostly on agile scrum teams.

But that's not all! For each area of measurement, I am presenting step by step procedure to make it concrete and applicable, based on my experiences. Whatever your current maturity level with regard to measuring your development process, you will learn from this book. Enjoy!

Agile

CHAPTER ONE

INTRODUCTION TO AGILE

Agile, the word means able to move quickly and easily. It is a way of dealing with, and ultimately succeeding in, an uncertain and turbulent environment.

The authors of the Agile Manifesto chose "Agile" as the label for this whole idea because that word represented the adaptiveness and response to change which was so important to their approach.

The modern history of Agile methodology starts in 2001 with Agile Manifesto postulated by the leading software developers who needed to create a clear-cut approach to the contemporary challenges offered by the ever-changing environment. Agile methodology is an umbrella term for a highly interactive and incremental approaches to software development based on the values and principles expressed in the Manifesto for a software development and the 12 Principles behind it. When you approach software development in a particular manner, it's generally good to live by these values and principles and use them to help figure out the right things to do given your context. Its the focus on the people doing the work and how they work together makes Agile different from other approaches to software development. Solutions evolve through collaboration between self-organizing cross-functional teams utilizing the appropriate practices for their context.

This is a particular approach to project management that is utilized in software development. Agile software development refers to software development methodologies centred round the idea of iterative development, where requirements and solutions evolve through collaboration between self-organizing cross-functional teams. It uses incremental, iterative work sequences that are commonly known as sprints.

CHAPTER TWO

VALUES &
PRINCIPLES.

Agile manifesto was formally produced by 17 developers during an outing on February 11-13, 2001, at The Lodge at Snowbird ski resort in Utah.

The developers, who developed a manifesto, called themselves the Agile Alliance. They were seeking a restructuring of the traditional software development processes that they saw as cumbersome, unresponsive and too keen and focused on documentation. They wanted to bring a balance and improve on client involvement. They were neither against the documentation nor favored it, as much as we used to, in traditional methods, which was never maintained and reused. They wanted to plan and limit the documentation to the required information. Their new approach to software development was "by doing it and helping others do it."

To make their view and priority clear, they created this document and called it "Agile Manifesto." When they built this document, they had no idea how quickly their ideas would spread beyond their industry, and in today's date, the Agile Manifesto is accepted globally.

The Agile Manifesto is a proclamation that articulates four fundamental values and twelve principles that its authors believe; software developers should use to guide their work of development.

Four core values of Agile.

The Agile Manifesto outlines 4 Core values which serve as a North Star for any team adopting an Agile methodology:

- Individuals and interactions over processes and tools
- Working software over comprehensive documentation
- Customer collaboration over contract negotiation
- Responding to change over following a plan

The General Principles of the Agile Method.

The Agile Manifesto proposes 12 principles that should be followed by agile methodologies:

1. Our highest priority is to satisfy the customer through early and continuous delivery of valuable software.
2. Welcome changing requirements, even late in development. Agile processes harness change for the customer's competitive advantage.
3. Deliver working software frequently, from a couple of weeks to a couple of months, with a preference to the shorter timescale.
4. Businesspeople and developers must work together daily throughout the project.
5. Build projects around motivated individuals. Give them the environment and support they need and trust them to get the job done.
6. The most efficient and effective method of conveying information to and within a development team is face-to-face conversation.
7. Working software is the primary measure of progress.
8. Agile processes promote sustainable development. The sponsors, developers, and users should be able to maintain a

constant pace indefinitely.

9. Continuous attention to technical excellence and good design enhances agility.

10. Simplicity--the art of maximizing the amount of work not done--is essential.

11. The best architectures, requirements, and designs emerge from self-organizing teams.

12. At regular intervals, the team reflects on how to become more effective, then tunes and adjusts its behaviour accordingly.

CHAPTER THREE

AGILE METHODOLOGY AT A GLANCE

Agile means are responsive. From that meaning, it is easy to interpret that this model will allow the team to respond with their concerns at any stage. Therefore, corrections can happen and then proceed with development. This will allow for modification as the entire process will be divided into iterations and hence each iteration is a small development life cycle. Since each cycle is independent of each other client can request a change at any stage. Agile is also called an incremental model. Several frameworks are used to implement the agile method. Scrum is the most used one in which the entire project is divided into sprints and the planning will happen per sprint and not for the whole project. What went wrong is discussed and the backlog is moved to the next sprint. The daily meeting will allow the team to discuss and continue. This leads to a transparent development process and there is no room for surprises from any stakeholder.

In Agile teams meet daily and hence all communication is weeded out. Everyone feels empowered and hence work with unity. Implementation happens in stages and hence the review of the end product is visible to the customer which helps them to fine tune their expectation. This means there is no need for additional investment in development and customer can add inputs in the middle of the project. People are important than the process so there is no rigid rule in what is to be done and when. Especially the quality team takes equal right like the development team and they can also share their views.

Even when the scope of the requirement is not known, the agile method allows the team to start the process. In short, the agile method can be used in small and medium-sized projects which require changes till the end of producing the end final product. Obviously, time and money are saved and there is no concern about untimely optimization.

CHAPTER FOUR

A PEEP INTO WATERFALL METHODOLOGY

Every development cycle begins with collecting the requirement, designing, developing, testing, deploying, and maintaining. This, when done in steps waiting for each step to get over, is called the waterfall method. Can you imagine how the water flows in a falls? It happens from the top to the bottom. The reverse will never happen. Similarly, going back to the previous step is not possible in the waterfall model.

Waterfall is a linear approach to software development. In this methodology, the sequence of events is something like:

- Gather and document requirements
- Design
- Code and unit test
- Perform system testing
- Perform user acceptance testing (UAT)
- Fix any issues
- Deliver the finished product

Overall, the linear-sequential life cycle model as the name implies each step occurs in sequence and easy to comprehend.

Managing deliverables are direct as each phase has a defined process. There is no overlapping of phases and allows completion in a phased manner. Small projects with the well-defined requirement and clear expectation can go with this model for a perfect outcome with minimal expenses.

Pitfalls of the waterfall model:

- This method has a major set back in the testing phase. It is not that the testing method is wrong but due to lack of chance to revisit will not only consume time but also entire work must be reworked. For instance, when testing and development happens concurrently, then fixing issues becomes possible. This facility is not available in this method which leads to chaos in huge projects.
- Working software model cannot be seen and the client has to wait until the end to see the result. Therefore, using this in object-oriented projects or complex projects will lead to risk.
- Dynamic requirements can never rely on this method as a change in the requirement is not allowed during the middle of the project.
- All this obviously conveys that the cost of implementing using the waterfall method is high in case of any issue cropping in any stage of development.

CHAPTER FIVE

ADVANTAGES OF AGILE SOFTWARE DEVELOPMENT.

There is a reason why the Agile methods are becoming mainstream. Agile is perfect for any project that requires a series of versions or iterations that need to be reviewed and improved on until the final product is ready for prime time. For example, instead of waiting six months for a deliverable that is either flawed or no longer meeting the current requirements, Agile lets you produce a first draft within as little as two weeks for immediate feedback—and from here you can improve upon each version until it's complete. Customers, vendors, and project managers alike all benefit from using the Agile Methodology. Traditional project implementation practices can be ineffective on complex projects with unclear requirements. This often led to projects being completed late, ineffectively, or not at all. In these types of projects, Agile can lead to greater success. The Agile software development methodology is one of the simplest and effective processes to turn a vision for a business need into software solutions. Agile is a term used to describe software development approaches that employ continual planning, learning, improvement, team collaboration, evolutionary development, and early delivery.

One thing that separates Agile from other approaches to software development is the focus on the people doing the work and how they work together. Solutions evolve through collaboration between self-organizing cross-functional teams utilizing the appropriate practices for their context. There's a big focus in the Agile software development community on collaboration and the self-organizing team. That doesn't mean that there aren't managers. It means that teams have the ability to figure out how they're going to approach things on their own.It means that those teams are cross-functional. Those teams don't have to have specific roles involved so much as that when you get the team together, you make sure that you have all the right skill sets on the team.

There still is a place for managers. Managers make sure team members have, or obtain, the right skill sets. Managers provide the environment that allows the team to be successful. Managers mostly step back and let their team figure out how they are going to deliver products, but they step in when the teams try but are unable to resolve issues.

The business agility is a recognition that in order for people in an organization to operate with an Agile mindset, the entire organization needs to support that mindset. Agile software development was never truly Agile until the organization changed its structure and operations to work in an uncertain environment.When most teams and organizations start doing Agile software development, they focus on the practices that help with collaboration and organizing the work, which is great.

Let's dive into some of the benefits that makes Agile methods valuable:

Higher Customer Satisfaction.

Throughout a project, there is an active involvement of everyone working on the project. By involving the different types of stakeholders in every step of the project, there is a high degree of collaboration between teams. This provides more opportunities for the team to truly understand the business' vision, deliver working software early, and frequently increases stakeholders' trust. You can demonstrate working functionalities to customers with every Sprint, allowing them to see continual progression. Since working functionalities are delivered faster, this means your customer will get a product to market faster, as well.

There is no substitute for demonstrating to the customer what we are building and getting their feedback regularly throughout the project. This is precisely what Agile projects do. Agility is a lever for developing customer satisfaction. It is its initial goal. The short development cycles make us often ask this question to our customers: what do you think of it? Depending on their feedback, we adjust our work. It is a guarantee that the project will be completed on time and budget and will perfectly meet the customer's request, as fluctuating as it may be.

Greater Agility and Reduced Risks.

The main reason why the Agile methods are called "Agile" is because of the iterative lifecycle which is designed to accommodate change. Customer's needs may change at any point of development. The iterative and incremental nature of the Agile planning process makes any of these sorts of changes much less disruptive than on traditional projects. Reworking the over-all project roadmap is relatively easy because it is based on rough order of magnitude estimates with very little accompanying detail. And because detailed planning is done just-in-time (for only a few weeks at a time), changes will cause little or no rework there as well.

With traditional project management methods where requirements are collected before work begins, a client could pay for an entire completed project, only to discover it isn't what they envisioned, which means lost time and lost money.

By developing in Sprints, vendors ensure a brief time between each feature development. This means any changes can be made rapidly, or new feedback can be integrated into the project almost immediately. Due to continual development, customers can feel confident that each final product will be closely aligned with their vision.

Faster ROI.

One of the distinct characteristics of software products is its dynamism and volatility. There's a continuous stream of innovative ideas in the market with previous ideas and solutions becoming obsolete at a similar pace. So, we cannot wait forever to build the right product before taking it to the market. The phase that transformed our whole process was when our traditional process was not able to get along with the frequent market demands. Every other week, we had to ship the products with changes. Another greatest customer benefits of the Agile Methodology is that projects implemented with this approach yield a rapid ROI. The keys to maximizing the business value of any method are low costs and high benefits. In Agile, Customers can identify the highest priority aspects of a project that have the greatest business value, and those tasks can be completed first. Customers can launch features or even their entire software program in a short timeframe by using the incremental way of development and after a few iterations, a functional product is ready for release.

The business value of Agile methods, when compared to traditional methods, proves to be very impressive and often the reality is that the customer's true needs can be met within a constrained timeframe or budget.

Productive development team.

Teams who follow an agile methodology are far more productive than teams following other practices. The guiding principles of agile were created so that teams can focus on one task at a time, with the ability to respond and pivot quickly as user needs and market forces change. The overarching idea of this approach is that if too many things are attempted at once, the team will ultimately fail from being overwhelmed and disorganised. Agile teams are known to be highly efficient at getting work done. Because Agile teams share a collaborative culture, efficiencies tend to have a ripple effect. The collaborative nature of an Agile development team means that each member of the team is learning from his or her peers continuously. Generalists become more generally capable, and specialists learn about each other's areas of specialty. In this way, each Agile project produces value that goes far beyond the product for the customer. Each team member becomes more and more capable with each Agile project.

High Product Quality.

The regular and continuous interaction between the customer and the developers have as their primary objective assuring that the product as built does what the customer needs for it to do. As long as the customer is effectively participating in the team, the developers will produce the right product. An iterative agile approach improves the quality and production time for software projects of all scope and size. Each iteration of a project is tested over and over to ensure it's working both during development and after release. Continuous integration and daily testing are fundamental aspects of the Agile development process.

Agile projects include the customer in all of the most important activities:

- The developers and the customer collaborate to define the high-level requirements (User Stories) and to maintain them throughout the project.
- The customer is present as the developers generate their rough estimates (e.g., Story Points) to answer questions about each requirement if necessary.
- The customer and the developers work out the order of development by considering the value of each feature to the customer as well as technical issues.

- The customer progressively elaborates the requirements details as the developers need them (mainly by responding to the developers' questions).
- The customer provides feedback to the developers about the product they are developing at least at the end of each iteration, and preferably more often.
- The customer and the developers collaborate to figure out how to adapt to each change as it is encountered on the project.
- Lack of Defects - The strong technical focus results in much better testing on an Agile project than in most other methods. Agile developers take responsibility for the quality of the code they write.

Increases project control and transparency.

Agile projects provide tremendous visibility and transparency into the overall progress of a project to any manager. For project managers or scrum Masters, aligning a project with customer needs is an obvious benefit to the Agile Methodology. In the past, it could be difficult for project managers to make the vision of a customer a reality. By constantly touching base with the customer, project managers have a clear sense of their vision and can implement feedback as soon as possible.

With the below level of visibility, managers will actually be able to manage software projects in a productive manner:

- The project's roadmap and what it means
- Changes to that roadmap and their implications
- Early indications of customer satisfaction.
- Early warning of problems.
- Impact of changing the project's budget or schedule.

Early and Predictable Delivery.

By using time-boxed, fixed schedule Sprints of 1-4 weeks, new features are delivered quickly and frequently, with a high level of predictability. This also provides the opportunity to release or beta test the software earlier than planned.

When vendors use the traditional waterfall approach to project completion, they often face challenges like slow progress and an overextended team. Using the Agile Methodology, vendors can do more with small teams, enhancing efficiency and maximizing profitability.

Good Project Management practice tells us that you must have a variable to manage in order to have a successful project. In the Agile methods, that variable is product Scope and Requirements. An Agile team will always deliver on time and on budget. The only question concerns precisely what will be delivered. This is the reason for the close participation of the customer in the project. That person's role is to ensure that the project meets their needs to the greatest possible extent within the project constraints.

CHAPTER SIX

WHICH IS THE RIGHT FIT FOR YOU?

Agile and waterfall methodologies are commonly applied to software development, and thus, project management as well. The main difference between agile and waterfall is that waterfall projects are completed sequentially whereas agile projects are completed iteratively in a cycle.

Both having their own set of advantages and disadvantages. Overall, both can be beneficial to a software development team. Which one to choose is highly dependent on the project type and circumstances.

We consider the following factors when considering which methodology to use:

Waterfall model

- If the requirement is well known and the client clearly mentions what they want, then go with the waterfall model and travel through each step one at a time.
- If the product is stable and no changes in scope in between then can be developed with the traditional model.
- If understanding technology is the key to development, then this model will help.

- When resources are available with ample time and expertise, then allot them in this way as they will implement without any downfall at any stage.
- Customer interaction is limited and projects that do not require their input can adopt this method.

Agile Methodology

- If the customer wants frequent and early opportunities to see the work being delivered, and to make decisions and changes throughout the development project.
- Use agile way when there is a need of dynamic environment. Every individual can share their view.
- If time to market for a specific application is a greater concern than releasing a full feature set at initial launch, Agile can more quickly produce a basic version of working software which can be built upon in successive iterations.
- If you want to produce more features in a shorter period.
- Development is often more user-focused, likely a result of more and frequent direction from the customer.
- If your project has few initial requirements and doesn't need to meet strict regulations, an Agile development methodology will result in project creativity and decreased time to market.
- If your organization doesn't have strict processes to follow and you have the luxury of being able to work flexibly, then Agile offers enough benefits to introduce the methodology.

CHAPTER SEVEN

AGILE PROJECT MANAGEMENT

Agile project management is an iterative approach to project management that focuses on breaking down large projects into more manageable tasks, which are completed in short iterations throughout the project life cycle. Teams that adopt the Agile methodology can complete work faster, adapt to changing project requirements, and optimize their workflow.

As the name suggests, the Agile allows teams to be better equipped to quickly change direction and focus. Software companies and marketing agencies are especially aware of the tendency for changes from project stakeholders to happen from week-to-week. The Agile methodology allows teams to re-evaluate the work they are doing and adjust in given increments to make sure that as the work and customer landscape changes, the focus also changes for the team.

Scrum is a powerful framework for implementing agile processes in software development and other projects. This highly adopted framework utilizes short iterations of work, called sprints, and daily meetings, called scrums, to tackle discrete portions of a project in succession until the project as a whole is complete.

Companies using agile are likely to leverage software geared to agile development in order to get the full benefits of this methodology.

Here are just some of the agile solutions available:

- Atlassian Jira + Agile: This is an agile project management tool that supports Scrum, Kanban, and mixed methodologies. This project management software comes with a comprehensive set of tools that help Scrum teams perform events with ease.
- Agilean: Agilean automates workflow management for small and midsize IT companies fitting different verticals. It is customizable and has 50 built-in templates.
- SprintGround: This is a project management tool created for developers to organize work and help them track progress.
- VersionOne: This project management solution is built to support the Scaled Agile Framework at all levels.

Key deliverables of Agile project management:

- Product vision statement: A summary that articulates the goals for the product.
- Product roadmap: The high-level view of the requirements needed to achieve the product vision.
- Product backlog: Ordered by priority, this is the full list of what is needed to be done to complete your project.
- Release plan: A timetable for the release of a working product.
- Sprint backlog: The user stories (requirements), goals, and tasks linked to the current sprint.
- Increment: The working product functionality that is presented to the stakeholders at the end of the sprint and could potentially be given to the customer.

CHAPTER EIGHT

AGILE FRAMEWORKS

Agile frameworks are characterized by building products that customers really want, using short cycles of work that allow for rapid production and constant revision if necessary. Agile software development methods support a broad range of the software development life cycle. Some methods focus on the practices (e.g., XP, pragmatic programming, agile modelling), while some focus on managing the flow of work (e.g., Scrum, Kanban). Some support activities for requirements specification and development (e.g., FDD), while some seek to cover the full development life cycle (e.g., DSDM, RUP).

Popular Agile frameworks used in current industry:

Kanban

A visual approach to project management where teams create physical representations of their tasks, often using sticky notes on whiteboards using various tools like Jira board. Tasks are moved through predetermined stages to track progress and identify common roadblocks.

Scrum

A PM methodology where a small team is led by a Scrum Master whose main job is to clear away all obstacles to completing work.

Work is done in short cycles called sprints, but the team meets daily to discuss current tasks and roadblocks that need clearing.

Extreme Project Management (XPM)

A PM methodology wherein you can change the project plan, budget, and even the final deliverable to fit changing needs, no matter how far along the project is.

Feature-Driven Development (FDD)

This framework is based on the idea of creating software models every two weeks. It also requires a separate development and design plan for every software model feature, making it more documentation heavy than some of the other Agile frameworks. Due to its rigorous documentation requirements, FDD is typically better for teams with advanced design and planning abilities.

In this book I will be explaining only about the Scrum framework as it is the most popular agile methodology used globally.

Scrum

CHAPTER NINE

Scrum - An Agile Framework

Introduction

Scrum is a widely-used, agile product development strategy—a collection of values, team roles, and rituals used in combination to create iterative work products.Anybody who has a complex project can benefit from using Scrum because it is a lightweight, iterative and incremental framework for managing those complexities.

Scrum was founded in the technology and software industries, but there are no limits to where Scrum can transform the world of work. Scrum and other agile frameworks have the power to transform project management across every industry in every business.

With Scrum, an entire project is split into a sequence of iterations called Sprints. Each Sprint is time-boxed for not more than one month and planned well in advance. Planning is completed not according to a set of prescribed tools, but according to the requirements as decided by the Scrum team. As such, a self-organizing and a cross-functional team is the backbone of the Scrum method. In order to ensure maximum cooperation among team members, face-to-face communication is encouraged. Also, the stakeholders and the technical team work in close collaboration, thereby ensuring the delivery of high-quality, working software.

When to adopt Scrum?

Scrum is best suited in the case where a cross functional team is working in a product development setting where there is a non trivial amount of work that lends itself to being split into more than one 2 – 4 week iteration.

Based on my experience, if the following aspects are met, then Scrum should be considered in your software development project.

- If the requirements are not clearly defined.
- If the probability of changes during the development is high.
- If there is a need to test the solution.
- If the product owner is fully available.
- If the team has self-management skills
- If the agreement between the business is defined under an open scope (Time and Materials) contract.
- If the client's culture is open to innovation and adapts to change

CHAPTER TEN

SCRUM VALUES

Scrum is more about behavior than it is about process. The framework of Scrum is based upon five core values. Although these values were not invented as a part of Scrum, and are not exclusive to Scrum, they do give direction to the work, behavior and actions in Scrum (when understood appropriately against the background of complexity and empiricism). Values drive behavior.

The Scrum framework helps each member determine what to contribute. Scrum values help each member determine how to deliver that contribution with an eye toward the long-term health of the team.The Scrum Team and its stakeholders agree to be open about all the work and the challenges with performing the work.

Ultimately the core of Scrum lies in living the Scrum Values. The five scrum values are:

Commitment

The Scrum value of commitment is essential for building an agile culture. Scrum teams work together as a unit. This means that Scrum and agile teams trust each other to follow through on what they say they are going to do. When team members aren't sure how work is going, they ask. Agile teams only agree to take on tasks they believe they can complete, so they are careful not to overcommit.

Great ScrumMasters reinforce a team's commitment when they facilitate sprint planning, protect teams from mid-sprint changes,

and deflect excessive pressure from product owners.
The keys to this are as follows:

- The product owner demonstrates commitment by making the best decisions to optimize the value of the product, not simply trying to please every stakeholder.
- The scrum master demonstrates commitment by upholding the scrum framework, which means we do not extend the sprint or other time-boxes under pressure to get to Done. And also demonstrates commitment by removing impediments that the development team cannot resolve themselves, rather than tolerating the status quo in the organization.
- The development team demonstrates commitment by creating an increment that meets their definition of Done and not something that is almost done.

Courage

The Scrum value of courage is critical to an agile team's success. Scrum teams must feel safe enough to say no, to ask for help, and to try new things. The team members have the courage to do the right thing and work on tough problems. The team members support each other in doing the right thing and in taking informed risks so that we may learn and improve along our path to greatness including:

- Admitting that nobody is perfect
- Delivering undone versions of product
- Sharing all possible information to help the team and the organization
- Admitting there are no perfect requirements for capturing and facing fast changes in reality

It's okay to be wrong, once, and having the courage to admit it. It's always appreciated by the team as it shows you are being transparent about the entire process which many people are invested in.

Focus

The Scrum value of focus is one of the best skills Scrum teams can develop. Focus means that whatever Scrum teams start they finish-- so agile teams are relentless about limiting the amount of work in process.

Everyone focuses on the work of the sprint and the goals of the development team. When we are dealing with complexity and unpredictability, focus is essential in order to get anything meaningful done. Because we focus on only a few things at a time, we deliver the most valuable items sooner.

If any endeavour big or small is to succeed, then applying strong focus to each element of work is paramount. Scrum allows teams to focus on important elements in smaller portions, meaning more focus can be given to each item in the process. When each team member is diligently focused on the work required for the Sprint and the goals of the entire Scrum Team, delivery of outcomes becomes fine-tuned and of high quality. Team members need to keep in mind that each item of work delivery they commit is valuable to the commitments agreed upon by the entire team.

Openness

Scrum teams consistently seek out new ideas and opportunities to learn. Agile teams are also honest when they need help. The empiricism of scrum requires transparency and openness by making known the arrangement of our work, our progress, our learning, and our problems. The team should be open to collaborate across disciplines and skills, to collaborate with stakeholders and the wider environment, to share feedback and learn from one another.

Openness facilitates empiricism and collaborative teamwork.

- Being open about our work helps create transparency to our progress.Without transparency, any attempts to inspect and adapt will be flawed.
- Openness enables team members to ask for help.
- Openness allows team members to offer help to each other.
- Openness enables team members to share their perspectives, feel heard by their peers, and be able to support team decisions.
- When our assumptions turn out to be invalid, openness helps us admit we were wrong and change direction. This applies to a feature we thought would be valuable. This also applies to how we chose to implement a feature in the product.

Respect

As self-organizing teams, we cannot do without respect for each other, in order to cultivate an engaged, productive, and humane environment for all.

Scrum team members demonstrate respect to one another, to the product owner, to stakeholders, and to the ScrumMaster. Agile teams know that their strength lies in how well they collaborate, and that everyone has a distinct contribution to make toward completing the work of the sprint. They respect each other's ideas, give each other permission to have a bad day once in a while, and recognize each other's accomplishments.

CHAPTER ELEVEN

Scrum Principles

Scrum principles are the core guidelines for applying the Scrum framework and should mandatorily be used in all Scrum projects. They are non-negotiable and must be applied as specified in the Scrum Body of Knowledge (SBOK Guide). Keeping the principles intact and using them appropriately instils confidence in the Scrum framework with regard to attaining the objectives of the project.

Following are the important scrum principles which are followed and incorporated while deploying a project:

1. Empirical nature of scrum

Empiricism means working in a fact-based, experience-based, and evidence-based manner.Scrum implements an empirical process where progress is based on observations of reality, not fictitious plans. Scrum also places great emphasis on mind-set and cultural shift to achieve business and organizational Agility.In Scrum, decisions are made based on observation and experimentation rather than on detailed upfront planning. Empirical process control relies on the three main ideas of transparency, inspection, and adaptation.

<u>Transparency</u>

Transparency allows all facets of any Scrum process to be observed by anyone. This promotes an easy and transparent flow of information throughout the organization and creates an open work culture. In Scrum, transparency is depicted through:

Artifacts - Project Vision Statement, Prioritized Product Backlog and Release Planning Schedule.

Meetings - Sprint Review Meetings and Daily Standup Meetings.

Information Radiators - Burndown Chart and Scrum board.

Inspection

Frequent inspection points built into the framework to allow the team an opportunity to reflect on how the process is working. These inspection points include the Daily Scrum meeting and the Sprint Review Meeting.Inspection in Scrum is depicted through:

- Use of a common Scrum board and other information radiators.
- Collection of feedback from the customer and other stakeholders during the Develop Epic(s), Create Prioritized Product Backlog, and Conduct Release Planning processes.
- Inspection and approval of the Deliverables by the Product Owner and the customer in the Demonstrate and Validate Sprint process.

Adaptation

Adaptation happens as the Scrum Core Team and Stakeholders learn through transparency and inspection and then adapt by making improvements in the work they are doing.Adaptation in Scrum is depicted through:

- Standup Meetings.
- Constant Risk Identification.
- Change Requests.
- Scrum Guidance Body.
- Retrospect Sprint Meeting.
- Retrospect Project Meeting.

2. Self-Organised Team

A self-organizing team is a team where team members get to decide among themselves who does what; the team gets to work on problems and have some power to remove their own blockages. Clearly, there are teams who are more self-organizing than others and teams which have more authority than others.

They has the autonomy to choose how best to accomplish their work, rather than being directed by others outside the team. Unlike traditional management principles, the self-organizing empowered teams are not directed and controlled from the top; rather they evolve from team members participating actively & collectively in all the Scrum practices and events. Some of the benefits of Self-organization are:

- Team buy-in and shared ownership.
- Motivation, which leads to an enhanced performance level of the team.
- Innovative and creative environment conducive to growth.

The ability for a team to self-organize around the goals it has been given is fundamental to all agile methodologies, including Scrum. In fact, the Agile Manifesto includes self-organizing teams as a key principle, saying that "the best architectures, requirements, and designs emerge from self-organizing teams."

How to Create a Self-Organizing Team?

From finding the right mix of people to setting up that group for success, there's a lot that goes into creating a self-organizing team. Ultimately, it comes down to three core steps:

- Training: Proper training can help satisfy many of the principles that self-organizing teams require.

- Coaching: Before becoming a true self-organizing team, groups need coaching. To provide this coaching, have a group start operating as a self-organizing team with a coach present every step of the way, offering guidance as needed.
- Mentoring: Once a team starts self-organizing, the journey has only just begun. Team members still require mentoring to grow their skills and maintain the balance of the team.This mentoring should also help with continuity by ensuring everyone grows together and remains motivated.

We can attribute the value of Agile self-organizing teams back to three core areas such as Increased efficiency, Continuous improvement and Improved problem solving.

3. Collaboration

Collaboration is what enables the whole team to be greater than the sum of its parts. Collaboration allows a team to work together to complete a product backlog item and then move on to deliver the next one. Collaboration allows a team to come up with effective solutions to complex problems.

If individuals are working separately, there is often a lot of partially done work at the end of a Sprint. This means the increment is not releasable. In order to enable effective solutions and deliver working software by the end of a Sprint, we must improve team collaboration. It is important to note the difference between cooperation and collaboration here. Cooperation occurs when the work product consists of the sum of the work efforts of various people on a team. Collaboration occurs when a team works together to play off each other's inputs to produce something greater.The core dimensions of collaborative work are as follows:

- Awareness — Individuals working together need to be aware of each other's work.

- Articulation — Collaborating individuals must partition work into units, divide the units among team members, and then after the work is done, reintegrate it.
- Appropriation — Adapting technology to one's own situation; the technology may be used in a manner completely different than expected by the designers.

Some of the benefits of Collaboration are:

- Minimization of change requests
- Risk Mitigation
- Increase in efficiency
- Continuous improvement

4. Value-based Prioritization

The process of prioritization involves determining what must be done now, and what can wait until a later date within in the project. Within the SCRUM framework, three factors influence prioritization:

- Value
- Risk or uncertainty
- Dependencies

By evaluating each of these factors, prioritization is done by the Product Owner when he or she prioritizes User Stories in the Product Backlog. The Prioritized Product Backlog contains a list of all the requirements needed to bring the project to fruition. It benefits projects through adaptability and iterative development of the product or service. More significantly, Scrum aims at delivering a valuable product or service to the customer on an early and continuous basis.

Thus, prioritization results in deliverables that satisfies the requirements of the customer with the objective of delivering the maximum business value in the least amount of time.

5. Time-boxing

Timeboxing is allotting a fixed, maximum unit of time for an activity. That unit of time is called a time box. The goal of timeboxing is to define and limit the amount of time dedicated to an activity. Scrum uses timeboxing for all the Scrum events and as a tool for concretely defining open-ended or ambiguous tasks. This ensures that Scrum Team members do not take up too much or too little work for a particular period and do not stretch their time and energy on work for which they have little clarity. Some of the benefits of Time-boxing are:

- Efficient development process
- Less overheads
- High velocity for teams

6. Iterative Development

Iterative Development is one of the main concepts to better Return on Investment (ROI). The Scrum framework is driven by the goal of delivering maximum business value in a minimum time span. To achieve this practically, Scrum believes in Iterative Development of Deliverables.The iterative model is more flexible in ensuring that any change requested by the customer can be included as part of the project. User Stories may have to be written constantly throughout the duration of the project.

Some of the benefits of Iterative Development are:

- It allows for course correction as all the people involved get better understanding of what needs to be delivered as part of the project and incorporate these learning in an iterative manner.

- The time and effort required to reach the final end point is greatly reduced and the team produces deliverables that are better suited to the final business environment.

CHAPTER TWELVE

THE SCRUM TEAM AND ROLES

The Scrum Team

The Scrum Team consists of a Product Owner, the Development Team, and a Scrum Master. Each of these roles in the Scrum has a very clear set of responsibilities which we will discuss in detail in the upcoming chapters of this book. Scrum Teams are self-organizing and cross-functional. Self-organizing teams choose how best to accomplish their work, rather than being directed by others outside the team. Cross-functional teams have all competencies needed to accomplish the work without depending on others not part of the team. The team model in Scrum is designed to optimize flexibility, creativity, and productivity. The Scrum Team has proven itself to be increasingly effective for all the earlier stated uses, and any complex work.On a Scrum team, everyone on the project works together to complete the set of work they have collectively committed to complete within a sprint, regardless of their official title or preferred job tasks. Given below are the 2 attributes of the Scrum Team:

- Scrum Team is Self-Organizing
- Scrum Team is Cross-Functional

Self-Organized Scrum Teams

These teams are self-reliant and self- sufficient in terms of accomplishing their work without the need for external help or guidance. The teams are competent enough to adopt the best of practices to achieve their Sprint Goals.

Cross-Functional Scrum Teams

These are the teams having all the necessary skills and proficiency within the team to accomplish their work. These teams do not rely on anyone outside the team for completing the work items. Thus, the Scrum Team is a very creative amalgamation of different skills that are required to complete the entire work item.Each team member may not necessarily have all the skills required to build the product but is competent in his/her area of expertise. Having said that, the team member need not be cross-functional but the team as a whole has to be.

The teams with high Self-Organization and Cross Functionality will result in high productivity and creativity.

Scrum Teams always have the following characteristics:

- Team members share the same norms and rules.
- The Scrum team as a whole is accountable for the delivery.
- The Scrum Team is empowered.
- It is working as autonomous as it is possible.
- The Scrum Team is self organizing.
- The skills within the Scrum team are balanced.
- A Scrum Team is small and has no sub-teams.
- The people within the Scrum Team work full time in the team.
- People are collocated.

The Scrum Team as a whole is responsible to deliver the committed delivery in time and with the defined quality. A good result or a failure is never attributed to a single team member but always the result of the Scrum Team.

The Product Owner

The Scrum product owner is typically a project's key stakeholder. Part of the product owner responsibilities is to have a vision of what he or she wishes to build, and convey that vision to the scrum team. This is key to successfully starting any agile software development project. The agile product owner does this in part through the product backlog, which is a prioritized features list for the product. The product owner is responsible for managing the product backlog in order to achieve the desired outcome that the team seeks to accomplish.This role exists in Scrum to address challenges that product development teams had with multiple, conflicting direction, or no direction at all with respect to what to build.

The Product Owner is the sole person responsible for managing the Product Backlog. Product Backlog management includes:

- Clearly expressing Product Backlog items.
- Ordering the items in the Product Backlog to best achieve goals and missions.
- Optimizing the value of the work the Development Team performs.
- Ensuring that the Product Backlog is visible, transparent, and clear to all, and shows what the Scrum Team will work on next.
- Ensuring the Development Team understands items in the Product Backlog to the level needed.

The Product Owner may do the above work or have the Development Team do it. However, the Product Owner remains accountable.He/She may represent the desires of a business in the Product Backlog, but those wanting to change a Product Backlog item's priority must address to the Product Owner.

For the Product Owner to succeed, the entire organization must respect his or her decisions. The Product Owner's decisions are visible in the content and ordering of the Product Backlog.

The Scrum Master

The scrum master is the role responsible for ensuring the team lives agile values and principles and follows the processes and practices that the team agreed they would use. The name was initially intended to indicate someone who is an expert at Scrum and can therefore coach others.The role does not generally have any actual authority. People filling this role have to lead from a position of influence, often taking a servant-leadership stance.

Scrum Master Service to the Product Owner :

- Ensuring that goals, scope, and product domain are understood by everyone on the Scrum Team as well as possible.
- Finding techniques for effective Product Backlog management.
- Helping the Scrum Team understand the need for clear and concise Product Backlog items.
- Understanding product planning in an empirical environment.
- Ensuring the Product Owner knows how to arrange the Product Backlog to maximize value.
- Understanding and practicing agility.
- Facilitating Scrum events as requested or needed.

Scrum Master Service to the Development Team:

- Coaching the Development Team in self-organization and cross-functionality.
- Helping the Development Team to create high-value products.
- Removing impediments to the Development Team's progress.
- Facilitating Scrum events as requested or needed.
- Coaching the Development Team in organizational environments in which Scrum is not yet fully adopted and understood.

Scrum Master Service to the Organization:

- Leading and coaching the organization in its Scrum adoption.
- Planning Scrum implementations within the organization.
- Helping employees and stakeholders understand and enact Scrum and empirical product development.
- Causing change that increases the productivity of the Scrum Team.
- Working with other Scrum Masters to increase the effectiveness of the application of Scrum in the organization.

The Development Team

Development Team consists of professionals (usually the developers and the QA's) who do the work of delivering a potentially releasable product at the end of each Sprint. A "Done" increment is required at the Sprint Review. Only members of the Development Team create the Increment.

Development Teams are structured and empowered by the organization to organize and manage their own work. The resulting synergy optimizes the Development Team's overall efficiency and effectiveness.

Development Teams have the following characteristics:

- They are self-organizing. No one (not even the Scrum Master) tells the Development Team how to turn Product Backlog into Increments of potentially releasable functionality.
- Development Teams are cross-functional, with all the skills as a team necessary to create a product Increment.
- Scrum recognizes no titles for Development Team members, regardless of the work being performed by the person.
- Scrum recognizes no sub-teams in the Development Team, regardless of domains that need to be addressed like testing, architecture, operations or business analysis.

- Individual Development Team members may have specialized skills and areas of focus, but accountability belongs to the Development Team as a whole.

Development Team size is small enough to remain nimble and large enough to complete significant work within a Sprint. According to the Scrum Guide, the development team should be between three and nine people and should have all the skills necessary to deliver product increments. The number of developers is usually dictated by the needs of the product and usually is between two and five developers in a scrum team.

CHAPTER THIRTEEN

WHAT MAKES A GREAT PRODUCT OWNER?

Role of Product Owner is very demanding and requires applying and adapting a wide range of skills, broad view of the subject knowledge and excellent communication, and multitasking skills. Great Product Owners act as a intrapreneurs (they behave like entrepreneurs while working in a large organization), they take full responsibility on maximizing the value of the product, they're visionaries, focus on creating valuable products that can make a difference on the market.

As the Scrum Guide clearly states, the product owner is responsible for maximizing the value of the product and the work of the development team. However, this statement represents an extensive list of duties and responsibilities—even an entire mindset that drives different dimensions: technical, business and design.A product owner has a clear and unique message of the strategy and tactics around the product. He/she is not only envisioning the product, but also strategizing it within the company and making decisions collaboratively with the team.The Scrum product owner is typically a project's key stakeholder. Part of the product owner responsibilities is to have a vision of what he or she wishes to build, and convey that vision to the scrum team. This is key to successfully starting any agile software development project. The agile product owner does this in part through the product backlog, which is a prioritized features list for the product.

Pragmatically, a great product owner is different from a good product owner in certain varieties of attributes, from a vision and strategic perspectives to a more tactical level:

Accountable

The product owner is primarily accountable for the product the development team is building and leveraging the most valuable backlog with user stories ready for the team.

A great product owner envisions the product in order to be in alignment with the mission and goals of the company. He/she develops an MVP (Minimum Viable Product), gathers the feedback with the customer, reflects and learns from it, then revaluates and adds more valuable features each time.

Agile Leader

A great product owner attends (or at least, tries) the daily standups 100 percent of the time; he/she also answers the three basic questions and is available to clarify any question from the team because he/she knows that a question is an impediment that needs to be addressed.

In sprint planning, the product owner shows an ordered set of user stories to be delivered by the team, declaring a real purpose for that particular sprint and answers as many questions as the team would like to ask.

The sprint review is when the product owner confirms and accepts the user stories accomplished in the sprint. The product owner may also take this opportunity to find gaps or take insights to leverage the product continuously. During the retrospectives, he/she listens to the team, contributes and then makes an action plan.

A great product owner doesn't push the team beyond their limits, he/she makes a room for the team to innovate and collaborate with the growth of the product. He/she makes the Scrum Master and development team awesome. His/her attitude makes the team feeling engaged with the product and part of it.

In addition to this, he/she clearly defines a purpose for any new resolution, feature, etc. An action without a purpose doesn't mean anything. He/she fosters the continuous improvement, finds ways for each individual to learn new things, new technologies, new frameworks, new practices and coaxes them to master their knowledge.

Backlog Refinement

A great Product Owner spends enough time at refining the Product Backlog. Backlog Refinement is the act of adding detail, estimates and order to items in the Product Backlog. The advise is to spend on average 10% of the capacity of the Development Team to refinement, the way it is done isn't prescribed and is up to the team. The Product Owner can involve stakeholders and the Development Team with refining the backlog. The stakeholders because it gives them the opportunity to explain their wishes and desires. The Development Team because they can clarify functional and technical questions or implications. This will ensure common understanding and increases te quality of the Product Backlog considerably.

Business-Centric

Maybe, this is the most complex topic for some product owners. A great product owner is capable of capturing terminologies, concepts, operations, and so forth, regarding the type of industry he/she is involved in.

Companies in the retail and payments space, just to give an example, have different business systems, hence the product owner should get the knowledge of these systems, rules, regulations, compliance and so on.

He/she drives and guides to deliver business value continuously to the customers based on a business model plan. It depends on each product, a business value can be related to the number of customers retention, new customers, the number of registered users, revenue generated, costs reduction, public/free services available, etc.

Designer

A great design delights the eyes of the customers, thereby a great product owner keeps the eyes open in any small piece that requires enhancements or adjustments. He/she is a perfectionist, satisfaction is something that remains all the time on his/her head.

A great product owner works with the SEO, UX & UI specialists to drive a friendly user experience in order to attract and retain the users. It's an ongoing process that requires experimentation, receiving feedback and collecting metrics to analyze the data, learn quickly and validate the hypothesis.

Innovative

A great product owner thinks differently, "out of the box," imagines a world that doesn't exist, experiments with new ideas and insights with the team, accepts failures, envisions the impossible, and gathers feedback from the customers, Scrum Master and development team.

Omnipresent

A great product owner has to be available to the team, communicate openly with each team member, understand their concerns, listen to them and guide them day by day according to the product vision and goals.

A product owner is easily accessible. The product owner job is all about communication, he/she ensures the team understands the vision and the "real" expectations are aligned with the team and stakeholders.

Organized

A great product owner inherits a certain amount of characteristics from the project manager role. In fact, his/her responsibilities also include controlling the budget and being organized with the roadmaps, set of features / epics, prioritized list of user stories, presentations, customer questionnaires, wireframes, designs and so on.

A backlog is built by the product owner and it consists of a set of elements:

- Who are the personas and target audience? Who are the market segments?
- What sort of features and benefits will the audience above pay for?
- When am I releasing each feature? Is there any event will drive it?
- How will the software architecture evolve?
- Are there any external dependencies to resolve?

Product Oriented

A great product owner understands that the word PRIORITY in practical terms doesn't have plural, because if you have, there isn't any priority. One of the most important words for the product owner is "no." Saying "yes" to a new feature request is easy.

The most important job for the product owner is deciding what not to build and own the consequences for that decision. A great product owner prioritizes what needs to be done by evaluating the business value and the amount of time required for building a feature.

Strategic

A good product owner knows how to gather requirements and translate into epics and user stories. Most of the time, he/she is on the tactical side.

A great product owner knows exactly how the business works, has open and frequent communication with the VPs, directors, managers, stakeholders and maybe even with the CEO. He/she strategizes the product with the sales managers, marketing people, legal department, security, compliance and so on.

He/she circulates the building to gather not only the requirements, but also the strategy and goals of the company to translate into a feasible roadmap that clearly identifies the targeted customer, primary goal and works with the team to set an expected delivery date.

Technical

A great product owner differentiates from a good product owner in terms of a very good technical knowledge in the field he/she is acting on. Is it feasible to have a product owner who is driving a cloud-based product without a deeper understanding of how a cloud architecture works and how to implement and release in a cloud environment?

Probably yes; however, a great one knows that every aspect of the product can benefit from different configurations from the cloud space.

CHAPTER FOURTEEN

HOW CAN BE SUCCESSFUL AS A SCRUM MASTER?

As per the Scrum Guide -

"The Scrum Master is a servant-leader for the Scrum Team. The Scrum Master helps those outside the Scrum Team understand which of their interactions with the Scrum Team are helpful and which aren't. The Scrum Master helps everyone change these interactions to maximize the value created by the Scrum Team."

Scrum Master is the name of one of the three roles in the Scrum project management framework. It is the most misunderstood role, as it has no counterpart in traditional project management methodologies. While the other two roles in Scrum (Product Owner and Development Team) take on most of the tasks traditionally performed by a project manager, the Scrum Master is entrusted with totally new duties.

A Scrum Master needs to do everything that keeps a team productive.This includes helping them to detect problems that hinder their work and also helping them to resolve these problems one at a time. It also includes helping them to work together as a team, omitting technical debt, deliver value frequently and so on.The Scrum Master is not a deep specialist, but deals with many deep specialists. He needs to be a generalist with a broad interest and understanding. He continuously needs to learn a wide range of subjects to be able to provide excellent services to his environment. A Scrum Master needs to learn about processes, change, frameworks, practices, soft-skills, psychology, software engineering, agile engineering practices and so forth.

What the Scrum Master is NOT:

- Scrum Master is NOT a project manager
- Scrum Master is NOT the boss
- Scrum Master is NOT responsible for talking to stakeholders
- Scrum Master is NOT the head that rolls in case of project failure
- Scrum Master is NOT the person calling everyone to the scrum meetings

Tasks of a Scrum Master:

- Watch the team and detect problems (process, personal, organizational etc).
- Conduct regular meetings to find sources for pressing problems and help the team to come up with actionable solutions.Example: In a retrospective every two weeks, the Scrum Master uses established methods to unearth and identify important problems hindering the work of the team. He coaches the team towards coming up with solutions and sees that the team implements these solutions during the next two weeks.
- Educate Product Owner and Development Team in their roles.
- Conduct Retrospectives.It's sole purpose is continuous process improvement.
  The Scrum Master moderates this meeting and helps the team to stay focused and keep improving.
- The result of any retrospective meeting are a handful of very specific and actionable tasks to be implemented to improve the process. The Scrum Master makes sure that each retrospective yields about 1–5 improvements to be done in the next sprint. Keep the number of action items small — tackling too many

impediments at once will lead to paralysis and to no improvements at all!

- The team or the Scrum Master can collect obstacles (so called "impediments"). This can help to keep track of issues in the work process and prioritize the most pressing obstacles to be tackled.
- Sprint Backlog - All work a team needs to do during a sprint is in the Sprint Backlog .Looking at this board and how cards/stories move (or not move) can give the Scrum Master hints towards possible impediments.
- Definition of Done - Many problems in the work process of a team are resolved by improving the Definition of Done.

Scrum Master needs to :

- Establish a good work process
- Work at a sustainable pace (no slowing of feature development over time)
- Keep everyone motivated and engaged
- Deliver and capture value as early as possible
- Don't waste time building the wrong thing or the thing wrong
- Protect the team, so they can do the work
- Remove obstacles, so the team can work productively

The Scrum Master needs to be an excellent teacher to transfer the Scrum knowledge, because knowledge leads to understanding. Teaching is fundamental to make the paradigm shift happen towards the empirical process control that Scrum implements.In addition to facilitating Scrum events, the Scrum Master creates and conducts workshops for a wide variety of purposes. The majority of development groups count multiple teams. This makes large group facilitation skills indispensable.

The Scrum Master acts as a change agent and knows how to reveal systemic impediments. He has the skills to bring about organizational change to improve product delivery.Scrum Masters has excellent soft skills because they work with people all the time. He/she supports team members, Product Owners and colleague-Scrum Masters in dealing with issues and with discovering and adopting (new) practices.

A Scrum Master knows how to start, build and grow Scrum teams.A Scrum Master can support and develop individuals and knows how to enable self-organization. A Scrum Master has the skills to coach anyone at any level of the organization.

Eight things that will benefit a good Scrum Master:

- Lots of experience! (Has done Scrum projects in the past)
- At ease with being inconvenient, annoying and a pita
- Ability to watch and listen
- No superior
- Servant leadership
- Empathy
- Communicative
- No fear (of superiors or being fired)

CHAPTER FIFTEEN

HOW TO BUILD A SELF ORGANIZING TEAM?

A self-organizing team is a team that has the autonomy to choose how best to accomplish their work, rather than being directed by others outside the team. Unlike traditional management principles, the self-organizing empowered teams are not directed and controlled from the top; rather they evolve from team members participating actively & collectively in all the Scrum practices and events. A self-organizing team has the autonomy to make some decisions and they also take ownership of their work, and consequently, the team is likely to become more self-motivated and seek to accept greater responsibility. And as a result, they deliver much greater value when self-organized. Some of the benefits of Self-organization are:

- Team buy-in and shared ownership.
- Motivation, which leads to an enhanced performance level of the team.
- The frequent interactions also lead to close team bonding and identification with project commitments.
- Innovative and creative environment conducive to growth.
- Active participation by all team members in all Scrum events.

Building a Self-Organizing team:

To build a self-organizing team, the organization should ensure that it provides the necessary infrastructure, training, and incentive system to keep employees motivated at work. Creating a self-organizing team can be considered a three-step process.

1. Training

Proper training can help satisfy many of the principles that self-organizing teams require. Specifically, hard skills training can ensure competency and provide the necessary framework to conduct tests that lead to regular improvements. Meanwhile, soft skills training can help lay the groundwork for high levels of communication, collaboration, commitment, and confidence.

2. Coaching

Before becoming a true self-organizing team, groups need coaching. They may require more support and guidance at the beginning. These are the indicators of your team getting more and more mature such as: Scrum ceremonies are productive, the team enjoys the work and members help each other, new ideas are forthcoming, and teams are pulling work for themselves. Finally, the role of the coach should diminish over time as team members learn how to take ownership and begin to collaborate with and trust one another in a self-organizing way.

3. Mentoring

Once a team starts self-organizing, the journey has only just begun. Assign mentors who can help the team go to the next level, so that the growth of the team will to be sustain in longer run. For example, job rotations can be an important aspect of keeping employees involved and of encouraging continuous learning, as this kind of mentoring could help with continuity by ensuring everyone grows together and remains motivated.

CHAPTER SIXTEEN

Scrum Events

The secret to scrum is simplicity, even in the face of complexity. And although scrum is simple at heart, it can be difficult to master. Scrum requires self-organizing teams that can quickly solve problems in unpredictable environments. In order to provide transparency and regular communication in the midst of such environments, scrum ceremonies are held. Scrum ceremonies are meetings that are unique to scrum teams.These Scrum ceremonies provide the pathway or the framework for all of the team members to accomplish all of their goals in a structured manner, help the team to set reasonable expectations and ultimately empower the team to communicate with each other so that the end results are perfect.

If due to some reason these ceremonies are not managed properly, they can mess up the project schedules and drown the value that the project was supposed to provide to the organization.

Each Scrum Project could have multiple Release Cycles and each release could have multiple sprints. There are several repeating sequence of meetings, to be held before, within and after the sprint cycle. Prescribed events are used in Scrum to create regularity and to minimize the need for meetings not defined in Scrum. All events are time-boxed events, such that every event has a maximum duration. Once a Sprint begins, its duration is fixed and cannot be shortened or lengthened. The remaining events may end whenever the purpose of the event is achieved, ensuring an appropriate amount of time is spent without allowing waste in the process.

Other than the Sprint itself, which is a container for all other events, each event in Scrum is a formal opportunity to inspect and adapt something. These events are specifically designed to enable critical transparency and inspection. Failure to include any of these events results in reduced transparency and is a lost opportunity to inspect and adapt.

Scrum defines four events (sometimes called ceremonies) that occur inside each Sprint:

1. Sprint Planning - Sprint planning is an event in the Scrum framework where the team determines the product backlog items they will work on during that sprint and discusses their initial plan for completing those product backlog items.
2. Daily Scrum - The Daily Scrum is held every day of the Sprint. At it, the Development Team plans work for the next 24 hours. This optimizes team collaboration and performance by inspecting the work since the last Daily Scrum and forecasting upcoming Sprint work. The Daily Scrum is held at the same time and place each day to reduce complexity.
3. Sprint Review - The Sprint Review is a Scrum Event or meeting, in which we inspect the work that was done during the Sprint, the Product Increment, together with our stakeholders.
4. Sprint Retrospective - The Sprint Retrospective is an opportunity for the Scrum Team to inspect itself and create a plan for improvements to be enacted during the next Sprint. The Sprint Retrospective occurs after the Sprint Review and prior to the next Sprint Planning.

And the one event that happens outside the sprint is :

1. Backlog Refinement or otherwise called as Backlog Grooming - Product Backlog refinement is the act of adding detail, estimates, and order to items in the Product Backlog.

Sprint

The Sprint is a timebox of one month or less during which the team produces a potentially shippable product Increment. Typical characteristics of Sprints:

- Maintain a consistent duration throughout a development effort.
- A new Sprint immediately follows the conclusion of the previous Sprint.
- Start date and end date of Sprint are fixed.

Sprints contain and consist of the Sprint Planning, Daily Scrums, the development work, the Sprint Review, and the Sprint Retrospective.During the Sprint:

- No changes are made that would endanger the Sprint Goal.
- Quality goals do not decrease.
- Scope may be clarified and re-negotiated between the Product Owner and Development Team as more is learned.

A Sprint can be cancelled before the Sprint time-box is over. Only the Product Owner has the authority to cancel the Sprint, although he or she may do so under influence from the stakeholders, the Development Team, or the Scrum Master.

A Sprint would be cancelled if the Sprint Goal becomes obsolete. This might occur if the company changes direction or if market or technology conditions change. In general, a Sprint should be cancelled if it no longer makes sense given the circumstances. But, due to the short duration of Sprints, cancellation rarely makes sense.

When a Sprint is cancelled, any completed and "Done" Product Backlog items are reviewed. If part of the work is potentially releasable, the Product Owner typically accepts it. All incomplete Product Backlog Items are re-estimated and put back on the Product

Backlog. The work done on them depreciates quickly and must be frequently re-estimated. Sprint cancellations consume resources, since everyone regroups in another Sprint Planning to start another Sprint. Sprint cancellations are often traumatic to the Scrum Team and are very uncommon.

Cancelling a sprint

The product owner can cancel a sprint if necessary.The product owner may do so with input from the team, scrum master or management. For instance, management may wish the product owner to cancel a sprint if external circumstances negate the value of the sprint goal. If a sprint is abnormally terminated, the next step is to conduct a new sprint planning, where the reason for the termination is reviewed.

Valid Reasons the PO Might Cancel A Sprint:

- A better technical solution is found that makes the current Sprint's activity throw-away work.
- A major technology change occurs.
- Market forces render the work obsolete.
- Fundamental and urgent external changes invalidate the Sprint Goal.

Why are these "valid" reasons for canceling a Sprint? Because they change everything about the Sprint.

Scrum – Sprint Lifecycle at a Glance:

1. Scrum process begins with a product owner. Product Owner creates a product backlog, a list of tasks and requirements the final product needs. The important part is that product backlog must be prioritized.

2. The Scrum Team makes estimates and arrangements for the workload based on the Product Backlog list in Product Backlog Refinement Meeting.

3. With the Product Backlog list, we need to hold a Sprint Planning Meeting for defining the sprint goal of this iteration (the time period of a Sprint is typically 1 to 4 weeks), then selected a list of user stories for the coming sprint which could fulfil the sprint goal. This subset of items from the product backlog becomes the sprint backlog.

4. Sprint Backlog is completed by the Scrum Team, each member is refined into smaller tasks according to the Sprint Backlog (the workload of each task can be completed within a few days).

5. Within the Sprint, a Daily Scrum Meeting is required and each of the meetings is time-boxed in about 15 minutes. Everyone must speak and face-to-face to interact with all members for reporting what you did yesterday, and commit what you want to accomplish today, and you can ask questions related to impediment or problems that you can't solve. Then, update your Sprint burn down Chart.

6. To achieve daily integration, that is, every day must have a version that can be successfully compiled and can be demonstrated; many people may not have used automated daily integration. If it passes, the unit test code is executed immediately. If all of them are passed, the version is released.

7. When all the user stories are completed, that is, the Sprint Backlog is completed, it means that a Sprint is completed. At this time, we need to conduct a Sprint Review Meeting (also known as a review meeting). The product owner and the customer must participate. Every member of the Scrum Team will demonstrate to them the working software they have completed, and this meeting is very important and must not be cancelled.

8. Finally, The Sprint Retrospective is held after the sprint review at the end of each sprint. During the retrospective, the team self-identifies elements of the process that did or did not work during the sprint, along with potential solutions. Retrospectives typically last 90 minutes and are there to help us incorporate continuous

improvement into our team culture and into our Sprint cadence.

Who attends what event in scrum?

Event	Event Owner	Product Owner	Scrum Master	Dev Team	Stakeholders and others
Sprint Planning Part I	Product Owner	Y	Y	Y	N
Sprint Planning Part II	Dev Team	Optional	Y	Y	N
Daily Meeting	Dev Team	N	Optional	Y	N
Sprint Review	Product Owner	Y	Y	Y	Y
Sprint Retrospective	Scrum Master	Y	Y	Y	N
Product Retrospective	Product Owner	Y	Y	Y	N

CHAPTER SEVENTEEN

Sprint Planning

A sprint planning meeting is conducted before the start of a sprint. The purpose of this meeting is to determine the sprint plan and set a sprint goal. Sprint planning includes agreeing on the number of backlog items in the sprint that is the responsibility of the development team and as well as to define the goal for the current sprint and sprint backlog.

During the sprint planning meeting, the product owner describes the highest priority features to the entire team. They will then discuss which stories the team will do in that sprint. The meeting should be attended by the whole team. If additional expertise on specific backlog items are required, then stakeholders can be also invited. The team may include the refinement sessions as well.

Below are some of the benefits of running a successful Sprint Planning meeting:

- Enables the Team to agree on the sprint goal and commitment.
- Enables task discovery, sign up, prioritization and estimation
- Creates the platform to communicate dependencies and identify team capacity to set and commit to an achievable sprint goal.

Each sprint begins with a sprint planning meeting. Typically, for a four-week sprint this meeting should last eight hours. For a two-week sprint, plan for about four hours. As a general rule of thumb, multiply the number of weeks in your sprint by two hours to get your total sprint planning meeting length. The following table illustrates the rule.

Total Sprint Duration	Sprint Planning Duration
1 Week	2 Hours
2 Week	4 Hours
3 Week	6 Hours
4 Week	8 Hours

How to conduct a Sprint Planning?

Sprint planning begins with a Capacity planning, which helps a team understand how many story points they are likely to accomplish within a sprint and takes into account company and personal time off, and commitments that impact the total time available for productive project work.

Then the Sprint planning is split into two sessions. In the first session, the product owner reviews the list of features and defines what needs to be built during the next sprint. The next session involves identification of tasks that need to be executed, in order to complete the build. The sprint planning meeting should yield the sprint goal and the sprint backlog.

Sprint Planning Meeting – Part I

Part one of the sprint planning meeting is a review of the product backlog items the Product Owner will ask the team to forecast and deliver. This is the time for the product owner to describe what she wants to make available by the end of the next sprint. During this part of the meeting, it is not uncommon for the team to banter back and forth with the product owner, asking clarifying questions and driving away ambiguity. By the end of sprint planning part one, the team will select a sprint goal: a one-sentence description of the overall outcome of the sprint. This helps later when questions about depth and breadth come up: if the work does not directly tie to the sprint goal, then it is not done during the sprint. The key activities to be conducted in Part I of the Sprint Planning Meeting are:

- During the first session the Product Owner presents the highest priorities of the Product Backlog to the team.
- Set the sprint goal or objective – Product Owner together with the development team think of the objective of the sprint.
- The team and the Product Owner collaborate to help the team determine what functionality can be delivered in the upcoming Sprint.
- The team commits to this Product Backlog at the end of the session – Selected Product Backlog.

Sprint Planning Meeting – Part II

During part two of the sprint planning meeting, the team decides how the work will be built. In this meeting the team will begin decomposing the product backlog items into work tasks and estimating these in hours. The product owner must be available during this meeting but does not have to be in the room. In fact, many teams find it helpful to work without product owner during this detailed part of the meeting. Knowing that the product owner is available yet not having her observing all the discussion about the best way to implement a feature can be freeing for many teams. Many teams find they enjoy discussing many implementation possibilities without worrying that the product owner will panic or misunderstand. If the product owner does remain in the room, the Scrum Master needs to take charge of this part of the meeting, keeping the team focused and free to explore possibilities without being limited by the product owner's own ideas or opinions. The key activities of the Part II of Sprint Planning are:

- During the second session of the meeting, the team plans how it will meet this commitment by detailing its work as a plan in the Sprint Backlog.
- Detail planning – Breakdown stories into tasks, ensure the team has separated the stories into tasks, as this will enable the team to consider everything that should be done to finish the stories. It's additionally great practice to make Testing as a different task.
- Estimating of the stories – Teams can do the measuring of the stories utilizing strategies like Planning Poker or T-Shirt Sizing and Allow team members to sign up for the work they choose and give an estimate as for how long each task will take to complete.

The Scrum Master ensures that the event takes place and that attendants understand its purpose. The Scrum Master teaches the Scrum Team to keep it within the time-box. At the end of the Sprint, the goal is to have a Potentially Shippable Product Increment (PSPI). We're trying to get something of incremental value done every Sprint. Sprint Planning answers the following:

- What can be delivered in the Increment resulting from the upcoming Sprint?
- How will the work needed to deliver the Increment be achieved?

The Sprint Planning meeting is carried out by the Scrum Master, who should ensure that everyone involved participates and understands the purpose. During this meeting the Scrum Master also makes sure that the Scrum Team respects the allocated time and they define two important things: a) the Sprint goal and the b) Team capacity.

Some best practices that will help you have an effective Sprint planning

<u>Set the Sprint Goal</u>

Coming up with a Sprint goal is an essential part of every Sprint planning. It should be specific and measurable and the result of a discussion between the Product Owner and the Development Team.The Sprint Goal is an objective set for the Sprint that can be met through the implementation of Product Backlog.

The sprint goal gives a short description of the end results, which should be realistic and comprehensible for everyone. Usually the goals are used for reporting to those who are not directly involved in the process – the same is with the Sprint Goal as well. The Sprint Goal is used to give an insight to the stakeholders about the process – what the team is working on, how is work progressing etc., but without going on further into product backlog item (user story) in details.

Sprint Goal can be decided on below factors:

- What do we want to achieve? This includes not only the isolated Sprint but also its contribution to the product as a whole.
- How can we achieve that goal? The team must go through each item and make sure everyone understands its requirements and can foresee possible impediments. This contributes both to the estimation and the Sprint goal clarity.
- How can we check whether we have achieved that goal? In other words, the definition of "Done", which is unique to your team and it's your job to make sure you're all on the same page.

Another important aspect to take into consideration is whether the goal you want to set is challenging enough. You don't want to create a goal that is too easy to achieve only to have a successful Sprint. After all, Scrum is all about the continuous improvement from iteration to iteration, and setting the bar too low won't contribute to the product nor the team. Make it challenging enough to bring out the best out of your team.

Once you Sprint goal is set, it will provide guidance to the Development team and help them set priorities to achieve that goal.

Arrange planning preparation meeting

Even though this is not a mandatory step, it can help a lot before the actual Sprint planning. You can discuss all the tasks that you intend to include during the Sprint planning with your team members.The key to the success of such a meeting is to make sure that every task is clear and precise.

Create subtasks

Once you've decided on priorities and which tasks you want to complete, it is time to create smaller tasks or subtasks that will help you complete them.

Don't take on too many tasks

It is easy to get too confident and take on too many tasks. While the Sprint goal should be a challenge for the team to fulfill, taking on too many tasks is counter-productive. Failing to deliver what the team agreed on, sets the stage for frustration and disappointment.

This can be solved by estimating how much time will be spent completing each task. You can and should use your previous experience completing similar tasks:

- What was the initial estimate?
- Did you deliver in that time?
- Were there unforeseen impediments?
- What are the chances of encountering them again?
- What other impediments can you predict?

CHAPTER EIGHTEEN

DAILY STAND UP MEETING

The Daily Scrum is a 15-minute time-boxed event for the Development Team. The Daily Scrum is held every day of the Sprint. At it, the Development Team plans work for the next 24 hours. This optimizes team collaboration and performance by inspecting the work since the last Daily Scrum and forecasting upcoming Sprint work. The Daily Scrum is held at the same time and place each day to reduce complexity.

The Development Team uses the Daily Scrum to inspect progress toward the Sprint Goal and to inspect how progress is trending toward completing the work in the Sprint Backlog. The Daily Scrum optimizes the probability that the Development Team will meet the Sprint Goal. Every day, the Development Team should understand how it intends to work together as a self-organizing team to accomplish the Sprint Goal and create the anticipated Increment by the end of the Sprint.

The structure of the meeting is set by the Development Team and can be conducted in different ways if it focuses on progress toward the Sprint Goal. Some Development Teams will use questions like:

- What did I do yesterday to meet the Sprint Goal?
- What will I do today to meet the Sprint Goal?

- Do I see any impediment that prevents me or the Development Team from meeting the Sprint Goal?

The Development Team or team members often meet immediately after the Daily Scrum for detailed discussions, or to adapt, or replan, the rest of the Sprint's work.The Scrum Master ensures that the Development Team has the meeting, but the Development Team is responsible for conducting the Daily Scrum. The Scrum Master teaches the Development Team to keep the Daily Scrum within the 15-minute time-box.

The Daily Scrum is an internal meeting for the Development Team. If others are present, the Scrum Master ensures that they do not disrupt the meeting. Daily Scrums improve communications, eliminate other meetings, identify impediments to development for removal, highlight and promote quick decision-making, and improve the Development Team's level of knowledge. This is a key inspect and adapt meeting.

CHAPTER NINETEEN

SPRINT REVIEW

At the end of the Sprint, the entire team (including product owner) reviews the results of the sprint with stakeholders of the product. The purpose of this discussion is to discuss, demonstrate, and potentially give the stakeholders a chance to use, the increment in order to get feedback. The Sprint Review is not intended to provide a status report. Feedback from the sprint review gets placed into the Product Backlog for future consideration.

The Scrum Master ensures that the event takes place and that attendees understand its purpose.

The Sprint Review includes the following elements:

- Attendees include the Scrum Team and key stakeholders invited by the Product Owner.
- The Product Owner explains what Product Backlog items have been "Done" and what has not been "Done".
- The Development Team discusses what went well during the Sprint, what problems it ran into, and how those problems were solved.
- The Development Team demonstrates the work that it has "Done" and answers questions about the Increment.
- The Product Owner discusses the Product Backlog as it stands. He or she projects likely target and delivery dates based on progress to date (if needed).

- The entire group collaborates on what to do next, so that the Sprint Review provides valuable input to subsequent Sprint Planning.
- Review of how the marketplace or potential use of the product might have changed what is the most valuable thing to do next.
- Review of the timeline, budget, potential capabilities, and marketplace for the next anticipated releases of functionality or capability of the product.

The result of the Sprint Review is a revised Product Backlog that defines the probable Product Backlog items for the next Sprint. The Product Backlog may also be adjusted overall to meet new opportunities.

CHAPTER TWENTY

SPRINT
RETROSPECTIVE

At the end of the Sprint following the sprint review the team (including product owner) should reflect upon how things went during the previous sprint and identify adjustments they could make going forward. The result of this retrospective is at least one action item included on the following Sprint's Sprint Backlog. This is at most a three-hour meeting for one-month Sprints. For shorter Sprints, the event is usually shorter. The Scrum Master ensures that the event takes place and that attendants understand its purpose.

The Scrum Master ensures that the meeting is positive and productive. The Scrum Master participates as a peer team member in the meeting from the accountability over the Scrum process.

The purpose of the Sprint Retrospective is to:

- Inspect how the last Sprint went with regards to people, relationships, process, and tools.
- Identify and order the major items that went well and potential improvements.
- Create a plan for implementing improvements to the way the Scrum Team does its work.

The Scrum Master encourages the Scrum Team to improve, within the Scrum process framework, its development process and practices to make it more effective and enjoyable for the next Sprint. During each Sprint Retrospective, the Scrum Team plans ways to increase product quality by improving work processes or adapting the definition of "Done", if appropriate and not in conflict with product or organizational standards.

Retrospectives aren't just a time for complaints without action. Use retrospectives to find out what's working so the team can continue to focus on those areas. Also, find out what's not working and use the time to find creative solutions and develop an action plan. Continuous improvement is what sustains and drives development within an agile team, and retrospectives are a key part of that.

By the end of the Sprint Retrospective, the Scrum Team should have identified improvements that it will implement in the next Sprint. Implementing these improvements in the next Sprint is the adaptation to the inspection of the Scrum Team itself. Although improvements may be implemented at any time, the Sprint Retrospective provides a formal opportunity to focus on inspection and adaptation.

CHAPTER TWENTY-ONE

REFINEMENT/ GROOMING

Product Backlog refinement or otherwise called as grooming is the act of adding detail, estimates, and order to items in the Product Backlog. This is an ongoing process in which the Product Owner and the Development Team collaborate on the details of Product Backlog items. During Product Backlog refinement, items are reviewed and revised. The Scrum Team decides how and when refinement is done. Refinement usually consumes no more than 10% of the capacity of the Development Team. However, Product Backlog items can be updated at any time by the Product Owner or at the Product Owner's discretion.

A crucial guideline in Scrum is that five to ten percent of every Sprint must be dedicated to Backlog Refinement. Refinement includes:

- Detailed requirements analysis
- Splitting large items into smaller ones (epics to User Stories)
- Estimation of new items
- Re-estimation of existing items

Product Backlog Refinement is not for PBIs selected for the current Sprint; it is for items in future Sprints. A good practice is to have at least two Sprints worth of work ready to go in the Product Backlog. Sprint Planning becomes relatively simple because the Product Owner and Scrum Team start the planning with a clear, well analyzed and carefully Estimated set of stories. If refining the

Backlog is not being done (or not being done well) Sprint Planning will involve a significant amount of questions, discovery and or confusion.

There are two critical parts of stories: getting them "Ready" and then getting them "Done" -- according to the agreed upon definitions of "Ready" and "Done." The refinement meeting is when the Scrum Inc Product Owner makes sure that stories are "Ready" so the team can immediately execute them when they are put into a current Sprint and get them to "Done." The Scrum Team may also invite people outside the Scrum Team to Refinement, such as experts or stakeholders, in order to gain technical, business or domain advice.

The Refinement Meeting:

Scrum Teams come together once per week to have their "Refinement Meeting". The Product Owner shares what Product Backlog items (user stories) need to be refined and the whole team discusses them. After the discussion (which can take a long time and often involves only a few), the planning poker cards are drawn to give an estimation to the Product Backlog Item.

Without condemning these type of meetings as a whole (they can be part of a healthy Refinement practice), they are not part of the Scrum framework events and often a couple of dysfunctions come into play here that lead to ineffective results:

- The Product Owner takes a lead in this meeting, drawing the ownership of refinement onto themselves.
- Endless discussions taking place, without really gaining more knowledge on the topic.Discussions involving only a couple of (senior) Development Team members.

Again, it may not be a dysfunctional meeting by default. Often teams need to gather to share insights and discuss effort to be able to empirically discover the work that can be handled. But it's something that I come across on a regular basis.The first step is to realize Product Backlog Refinement is not a meeting, but a series of different activities. Meetings can be included. Every member of the Scrum Team is responsible for Product Backlog Refinement:

- The Product Owner: building the right thing.
- The Development Team: building the thing right.
- The Scrum Master: ensuring feedback and empiricism throughout these activities.

Let's look at different activities that might be helpful in regards to refinement from the perspective of the different Scrum roles.

The Product Owner :

- Setting up a product vision.
- Creating a product road map.
- Making a storyboard.
- Creating personas for the product.
- Defining assumptions that can be validated (i.e. using an MVP by the Development Team).
- Defining acceptance criteria or satisfaction criteria.
- Organizing a user story writing workshop (with customers and stakeholders!).
- Talking to customers and stakeholders about their use of the product.
- Doing market research.
- Setting out goals to achieve.

The Development Team :

- Finding creative solutions for meeting the Sprint Goal that can be worked out during the Sprint.
- Estimating, so there is an idea of the work that can be done in a Sprint.

- Discussing and collaborating with other Development Team members (possible also of other teams) to establish sound architectural guidelines.
- Do little experiments / MVP's to validate assumptions and test hypothesis.
- Document possible solutions to work out in the Sprint.
- Set up measurements for the product to measure behavior of customers.
- Slicing large PBI's up into smaller functional units of work.

The Scrum Master :

- Facilitate Product Backlog Refinement workshops.
- Facilitate estimation workshops on value and effort.
- Teach the importance of shared responsibility in Product Backlog Refinement.
- Teach on metrics that can help the Development Team raise their transparency on the way they deliver and collaborate, i.e. lead time, cycle time, flow, time to learn, time to market etc.
- Teach and coach the Product Owner and Development Team on self-organizing (anti) patterns, like the example given earlier.
- Help the Development Team in slicing PBI's in various ways, while still being able to deliver a "Done"-increment within the Sprint.

CHAPTER TWENTY-TWO

RELEASE PLANNING AND CAPACITY PLANNING

Release Planning.

Release planning is about making the scope, date, and budget trade-offs for incremental deliveries. It is all about 'high-level planning' of multiple sprints (three to twelve iterations). Most of the times, it is sensible and important to carry out Initial Release Planning after product planning and before beginning the first Sprint related to the Release.

At this point, you can make an initial release plan showing a balance between how much can be built in the release against when the release will be available. You can generate and estimate a sufficient number of product backlog items to get an idea of when you can deliver a fixed set of features.You can draw a release line through the product backlog to visualize the release. All the items below a line are not planned for a release, whereas all the items above a line are planned for the release. This release line can move up and down in the product backlog as you get in-depth knowledge of the product.

Now, you can easily tie up the product roadmap with the product backlog. This provides a detailed specification of the contents. Product roadmap describes the incremental way of building a product and delivering in time along with some crucial factors that help in each release. A product roadmap is very useful while developing any product having more than one release.

Release planning involves the complete Scrum team and the Stakeholders. At some point, the involvement of all these people is necessary to maintain a good balance between a value and quality.

Timing and Purpose of Release planning

Release Planning event happens frequently, during every sprint activity. Logically, initial release planning follows product-level planning. The aim of product planning is to plan what will be the final product.

The purpose of release planning is to find out the next logical step in achieving a product goal. Many organizations implementing Scrum create an introductory release plan through initial release planning. The initial release planning lasts a day or 2-days. This timing may vary based on the size of the release and the team members' familiarity with the concepts that are being created.

How Release Planning works?

Release planning refers to as longer-term planning. It enables to answer the following questions like:

- When will we be done?
- How much will this cost?
- Which features can I get by the end of the year?
- Release Planning includes a balance between the customer value and complete product's quality against the constraints like scope, budget and time.

Every organization implementing Agile must decide its own cadence during a release of the product. Some organizations decides to release every sprint, while others combine multiple sprints into one release and others release just after the completion of each feature, this practice is called continuous deployment or continuous delivery. Let's understand the different release cadences, that are made up of multiple sprints, occur every sprint, and occurs multiple times each sprint.

Excecution Release Planning is below:

The inputs to release planning include:

- The output from the Product planning (the product vision, high-level product backlog, and product roadmap)
- The velocity of the team/teams

In Release Planning, one activity includes a confirmation of the constraints like scope, date, and budget during a release and auditing these constraints to check whether any changes are needed, given a passage of time and what we presently think about the product and its release. Another activity in release planning is product backlog grooming (product backlog refinement). This includes creating, estimating and prioritizing the product backlog items.

These activities can happen at various points in time, as follows:

- Before initial release planning, but after product planning
- As a part of the initial release planning activity
- During each sprint
- Each release must have a very much characterised set of Minimum Releasable features (MRFs).

Output of Release Planning process:

The outcome of the Release Planning is 'release plan'. The Release plan communicates a level of accuracy, when we will finish the product, what features we will get at the end, and how much will be the cost. Also, the release plan communicates the desired MRFs for a release.

Capacity Planning.

Capacity planning is usually done at the begining of the sprint planning.

Capacity planning is a process that balances the available hours of teams against what the project needs. Capacity in this case is the most work that can be done over a certain timeframe.

It's a bit of a juggling act that has to keep several balls in the air, such as the availability of the team, the money in the budget for those hours and what is demanded by the client, stakeholder or customer. Capacity and project planning obviously go hand-in-glove. Planning is how one schedules the hours of the team members so that the work gets done in time.

At the start of the capacity planning meeting, go around the room and ask team members for available days, as well as how many hours or what percent of time they expect to contribute to the project. Use a spreadsheet to track this information on a per-person basis so that each member can make sure their availability is reflected accurately. Set up the spreadsheet to calculate automatically the total productive team hours so that, at the end of the exercise, the team is ready to launch into reviewing, estimating and committing to stories for the sprint.

Capacity planning helps a team understand how many story points they are likely to accomplish within a sprint and takes into account company and personal time off, and commitments that impact the total time available for productive project work.

How to calculate Capacity?

At the root of Agile capacity planning is a simple equation: Number of team members multiplied by number of days in the sprint multiplied by number of productive hours in a day. In most cases, more complex parameters are considered in the capacity planning equation, but this calculation can be used for well-jelled teams that have achieved a consistent velocity of story points completed per sprint. Even with these ideal teams, additional parameters need to be taken into account if a team member is unavailable for some or all of the sprint, if members are added or leave the team, and if technology and domain knowledge change ahead of the next sprint.

Person Days in a Sprint :

The number of person days in a sprint is determined by the first part of the equation: number of team members multiplied by number of days in the sprint. For example, a three-week sprint with no holidays has 15 days; if there are six team members, there is a maximum of 90 person days in the sprint. In most sprints, company holidays and events, team members' planned time off, training, travel and other corporate obligations impact the total number of person days. A one-day company holiday decreases the number of days in the sprint to 14, and the total number of person days to 84. If a team member takes a week-long vacation (five days), the 84 days are decreased to 79. If two more employees each take two days of training (four days), the 79 days fall to 74.

Number of Productive Hours:

The number of productive hours in a day refers to the number of hours team members could, realistically, be expected to work actively on the project. Start by assuming that any given team member is available a maximum of 75 percent of a day (typically six hours); the remaining time is spent reading and responding to email, in meetings and dealing with other tasks that are not related to the story work. Some teams have members who work across multiple teams and who are available for even fewer hours during a sprint; availability for that team member can be altered either by changing the number of available days or the number of available hours. Even adding and educating a new team member can impact productive hours; the new member will start at less than full capacity as he comes up to speed, while another team member is likely to see a decrease in available hours as she assists the new member.

CHAPTER TWENTY-THREE

WHAT IS DOR AND DOD?

DoR

Definition of Ready(DOR) means a clearly defined Story with a

- Clear set of Development Requirement
- Clear Statement on the Business Value that will be resulted from the implementation of this Story (or the Product Increment this Story belongs to).
- Clear listing of Pre-Dev enablers that need to be added to the Story prior to Dev work (such as UXD wireframes, Visualization Designs, Prototypes, Mock shots, Simulation Data, Test Data and so on).

DoR is created to make a story ready to be picked up by the Dev team.Development Team decides if a Story is Ready for selection into the new Sprint.If they decide a Story presented by the PO is Not Ready, they can ask PO to provide the needed clarification and details (and/or examples, mock images or prototypes).Development Team should NEVER be forced to bring in Stories that they did not commit to deliver.Backlog Refinement sessions, even though they are not officially part of Scrum process, have empirically proven to be the best opportunity for both parties to review the Readiness of the Stories and to ask for clarifications.PO would then have time to continue to find answers to Development Teams' questions on the requirements and clarifications.

DoR also requires the Story to meet the following criteria:

- Estimation should be done by the Development team.
- It should avoid any pending dependencies to any external resources or elements during the Sprint (i.e. The Development Team should not have to depend to someone outside their team to deliver any piece before they can take on the Story).
- In cases where it is inevitable that a live external dependency is going to exist and follow a Story through the Sprint, proper adequate coordination with the external dependency must be arranged and closely tracked to avoid disruption to the work during the Sprint (let's not forget that we need to consider time needed for testing once the Dev is completed and a delay imposed by external dependencies can damage our commitment to deliver).

DoD

Definition of Done (DoD) is a mutual agreement between the Development Team and PO on what constitutes a Story that is ready for Release.Some organizations have pre-defined DoDs for a variety of Story types. They may even be defined at departmental levels.In other cases no such pre-definition is in place and it is up to the Scrum Team to establish that agreement.It is important for all Scrum Teams working within the same department or being in any sort or interdependent working relationship to establish and use the same DoD.

DoD can be defined as a blanket cover for all Story types, or can be more granular to provide a different set for any specified

Story types.DoD is a qualifying status for a Release Ready Product Increment.

Based on what it means for that Scrum Team (or their department) to be considered Release Ready, it should contain cover:

- Completion of Development.
- Completion of Code Review.
- Completion of Testing: Unit Testing, Regression Testing, Integration Testing, Functional Testing, Non-functional Testing, User Acceptance Testing, Usability Testing, Stability Testing, Stress Testing etc or any other QA work .
- Meeting all Acceptance Criteria (for that specific Story or group of Stories).
- SLA (Service Level Agreements).
- Performance (meeting certain metrics).
- Compliance (adhering to certain constraints or coverage).
- Information Security Audit (if needed).
- Accessibility Audit (if needed).
- Technical Debt (either to lessen or at least not add to).
- PO Accepted the Product Increment (and deemed as Releasable).
- Stakeholders Sign-off (or Acceptance of any kind): would includes: Demo is prepared, Demo is presented, Approval Received.
- Knowledge Center updated (or manuals or training materials and such).
- Sprint Goals are all check marked.
- Build is complete and its free from bugs.
- Build is successfully promoted to the Production Environment.
- Release Notes are prepared and provided.
- Infrastructure Change Documents provided.
- Operations hand-over is completed and they are ready to take over after the Release. (This may also need to extend to other areas as well, such as Call Center or Customer Support).

CHAPTER TWENTY-FOUR

SCRUM LIFE CYCLE

Scrum lifecycle is a number of consecutive steps and iterative stages that should be performed during the realization of any Scrum project.

Step 1: Creation of a scrum project

Once you create and log in to an account in your software tools like Jira ,Trello, Azure devops etc, you can create a project. When you're prompted to select a project template, select Scrum.

Once you've created your project, you will land on the empty backlog. The backlog is also known as the product backlog and contains an ongoing list of your team's potential work items for the project.

Step 2: Create user stories in the backlog

Create a few user stories with the quick create option on the backlog. If you don't have user stories in mind, just create sample stories to get started and see how the process works.

Once you've created a few user stories, you can start prioritizing them in the backlog. You rank or prioritize your stories by dragging and dropping them in the order that they should be worked on. Or in some tools we categorise them by giving the priority in numbers.

These are just the starting stories for your project. You will continue to create stories for the project's lifetime. This is because agility involves continuously learning and adapting.

Step 3: Create a sprint

Create your first sprint in the backlog so you can start planning the sprint. Sprints are one, two, or four weeks long. It's up to the team to determine the length of a sprint — we recommend starting with two weeks. That's long enough to get something accomplished, but not so long that the team isn't getting regular feedback. Once a sprint cadence is determined, the team perpetually operates on that cadence. Fixed length sprints reinforce estimation skills and predict the future velocity for the team as they work through the backlog.

Step 4: Sprint planning meeting

In this meeting, the entire team discusses the sprint goal and the stories in the prioritized product backlog. Then the development team commits to completing a certain number of stories in the sprint. These stories and the plan for completing them become what is known as the sprint backlog.You can also add more details to the stories or click the create subtask icon to further break down the work of the story.

Drag the stories agreed to in the sprint planning meeting into the sprint that you just created. This is your sprint backlog.

Attendees required: development team, scrum master, product owner.

When: At the beginning of a sprint.

Duration: Usually two hours per week of iteration – e.g. a two-week sprint kicks off with a four-hour planning meeting. The meeting ends when its purpose has been achieved.

Purpose: Plan the work of the sprint. The team agrees to the sprint goal and the sprint backlog.

Step 5: Start the sprint

Add a duration of the sprint and start and end dates. The start and end dates should align to your team's schedule. For example, some teams start sprints on a Monday and then end on a Friday morning in the next week. Other teams decide to start and end their sprints mid-week. It's up to you! If you're unsure how long your sprints should be, we recommend trying two weeks.

Add the sprint goal as agreed to in the sprint planning meeting.

Once you start your sprint, you will be taken to the Active sprints tab in the project.This is where your team will work to pick up items from the to-do column and move them into in-progress and eventually, done.

Step 6: Daily standup meetings

After your sprint has started, have your team meet daily, typically in the morning, to review what everyone is working on. The purpose of this is to see if anyone on your team is experiencing any roadblocks towards the completion of sprint tasks.

Attendees : development team.

When: Once per day, typically in the morning.

Duration: No more than 15 minutes.

Purpose: The daily standup is designed to inform everyone quickly of what's going on across the team and to plan the work of the day. It's not a full status meeting.

Have each team member answer the following questions:

- What did I complete yesterday?
- What will I work on today?
- Am I blocked by anything?

You can use the active sprints of your scrum board during the daily standup, so that each member can view the tasks they're working on.

Step 7: View the Burndown Chart

The Burndown Chart is automatically updated as you complete work items.

A Burndown Chart shows the actual and estimated amount of work to be done in a sprint. The horizontal x-axis in a Burndown Chart indicates time, while the vertical y-axis typically indicates story points.Use the Burndown Chart to track the total work remaining for a sprint, and to project the likelihood of achieving the sprint goal. By tracking the remaining work throughout the iteration, a team can manage its progress and respond accordingly.

Anti-patterns to watch for:

- The team finishes early sprint after sprint because they aren't committing to enough work.
- The team misses their forecast sprint after sprint because they're committing to too much work.
- The burndown line makes steep drops rather than a more gradual burndown because the work hasn't been broken down into granular pieces.
- The product owner adds or changes the scope mid-sprint.

Step 8: View the Sprint Report

At any point during or after the sprint, you can view the Sprint Report to monitor the sprint.The Sprint Report includes the Burndown Chart, and lists the work completed, work not completed, and any work added after the sprint started.

Step 9: Sprint Review meeting

The sprint review, or sprint demo, is a sharing meeting where the team shows what they've shipped in that sprint. Each sprint usually produces a working part of the product called an increment.This is a meeting with a lot of feedback on the project and includes a brainstorming session to help decide what to do next.

Attendees : Development team, Scrum master, Product owner, Stakeholders.

When: Typically on the last day of the sprint.

Duration: Typically two hours for a two-week sprint.

Purpose: Inspect the increment and collaboratively update the product backlog.

Questions to ask:

- Did the team meet the sprint forecast?
- Was there work added or removed during the middle of the sprint?
- Did any work not get completed within the sprint?
- If so, why?

Step 10: Sprint Retrospective meeting

Document your retrospective somewhere.

Attendees: Development team, Scrum master,Product owner.

When: At the end of an iteration.

Duration: Typically 90 minutes for a two-week sprint.

Purpose: The team inspects itself, including its processes, tools and team interaction. Improvement issues are often added to the next sprint's backlog.

Questions to ask:

- What did we do well during the sprint?
- What could we have done better?
- What are we going to do better for next time?

Even if things are going well across the team, don't stop doing retrospectives. Retrospectives provide ongoing guidance for the team to keep things going well.

Step 11: Complete the sprint

At the end of the sprint, you must complete it.If the sprint has incomplete issues, you can:

- Move the issue(s) to the backlog.
- Move the issue(s) to a future sprint.
- Move the issue(s) to a new sprint, which Jira will create for you.

CHAPTER TWENTY-FIVE

SCRUM ARTIFACTS

Scrum Artifacts provide key information that the Scrum Team and the stakeholders need to be aware of for understanding the product under development, the activities being planned, and the activities done in the project.Agile has its own particular byproducts that emerge from the scrum experience of planning, development, tracking, and iteration of tasks to build software.The following Artifacts are defined in Scrum Process Framework.

Product Vision

The Product Vision is an artifact to define the long-term goal of the project/product. It sets the overall direction and guides the Scrum Team. Everyone should be able to memorize the Product Vision. Therefore, it must be short and precise.

Sprint Goal

A sprint goal is a shared high-level objective that describes the key outcome for each sprint that a Scrum team undertakes. In the same way that a product vision guides the longer-term direction of a product, the sprint goal guides the development team on why it is building the current increment. It also covers why it is worthwhile undertaking the sprint, and what value it will deliver to the product owner.

As per the Scrum Guide, the responsibility for crafting a Sprint Goal is for the Scrum Team. It is however in large part of interest to the Product Owner to support this process by having clear business goals for the coming Sprint, which can also make ordering the Product Backlog a lot easier by providing Focus.

Product Backlog

A Product backlog lists and prioritizes the task-level details required to execute on the strategic plan set forth in the roadmap. The backlog should communicate what's next on the development team's to-do list as they execute on the roadmap's big-picture vision. Typical items in a product backlog include user stories, bug fixes, and other tasks.

Product backlog owned by the Product Owner (PO) which consists of a lists all features, functions, requirements, enhancements, and fixes that constitute the changes to be made to the product in the future releases.

Typically, the requirements of a product keep changing, i.e. change in business requirements, market conditions, or technology. Thus, product backlog is consistently updated to reflect what the product needs to be most useful to the target users.

The product backlog and the business value of each product backlog item is the responsibility of the product owner. The effort to deliver each item is estimated by the development team in story points, or time.Every team should have a product owner, although in many instances a product owner could work with more than one team.The product owner is responsible for maximizing the value of the product. The product owner gathers input and takes feedback from, and is lobbied by, many people, but ultimately makes the call on what gets built.

On short, the product backlog:

- Captures requests to modify a product—including new features, replacing old features, removing features, and fixing issues
- Ensures the development team has work that maximizes business benefit to the product owner.

Typically, the product owner and the scrum team work together to develop the breakdown of work; this becomes the product backlog, which evolves as new information surfaces about the product and about its customers, and so later sprints may address new work.

Sprint Backlog

The sprint backlog is a list of tasks identified by the Scrum team to be completed during the Scrum sprint. This list is derived by the scrum team during the sprint planning meeting by progressively selecting product backlog items in priority order from the top of the product backlog until they feel they have enough work to fill the sprint. Most teams also estimate how many hours each task will take someone on the team to complete.The development team should keep in mind its past performance assessing its capacity for the new-sprint, and use this as a guideline of how much 'effort' they can complete.

It's critical that the team selects the items and size of the sprint backlog. Because they are the people committing to completing the tasks, they must be the people to choose what they are committing to during the Scrum sprint.

The product backlog items may be broken down into tasks by the development team.Tasks on the sprint backlog are never assigned to team members by someone else; rather team members sign up for tasks as needed according to the backlog priority and their own skills and capacity. This promotes self-organization of the development team and developer buy-in.

The sprint backlog is the property of the development team, and all included estimates are provided by the development team. Often an accompanying task board is used to see and change the state of the tasks of the current sprint, like to do, in progress and done.

Once a sprint backlog is committed, no additional work can be added to the sprint backlog except by the team. Once a sprint has been delivered, the product backlog is analyzed and reprioritized if necessary, and the next set of functionality is selected for the next sprint.

Definition of Done

The definition of done (DoD) is when all conditions, or acceptance criteria, that a software product must satisfy are met and ready to be accepted by a user, customer, team, or consuming system. We must meet the definition of done to ensure quality. It lowers rework, by preventing user stories that don't meet the definition from being promoted to higher level environments. It will prevent features that don't meet the definition from being delivered to the customer or user.

The most common use of DoD is on the delivery team level. Done on this level means the Product Owner reviewed and accepted the user story. Once accepted, the "done" user story will contribute to the team velocity. You must meet all the defined criteria, or the user story isn't done.

User Story DoD Examples:

- Unit tests passed
- Code reviewed

- Acceptance criteria met
- Functional tests passed
- Non-Functional requirements met
- Product Owner accepts the User Story

Increment

Product Increment is one of the important deliverables or artefacts of Scrum. Product Increment is the integration of all the completed list of Product Backlog items during the sprint. As the name suggests, Product Increment goes on getting incremented in the subsequent sprints. So, in a particular sprint, the Product increment is the integration of all the completed list of Product Backlog Items whereas in a Project, Product Increment is the integration of all the completed list of Sprint backlog items. With each sprint, the product increment increases in terms of delivered functionality.

At the end of a Sprint, the new Increment must be "Done," which means:

- It must meet the Scrum Team's Definition of "Done."
- It must be in usable condition regardless of whether the Product Owner decides to actually release it.

The Burndown Chart

The Scrum Burndown Chart is a visual measurement tool that shows the completed work per day against the projected rate of completion for the current project release. Its purpose is to enable that the project is on the track to deliver the expected solution within the desired schedule. It shows the total effort against the amount of work we deliver each iteration.

The rate of progress of a Scrum Team is called "velocity". It expresses the amount of e.g. story points completed per iteration. An import rule for calculating the velocity is that only stories that are completed at the end of the iteration are counted. Counting partially finished work (e.g. coding only - test missing) is strictly forbidden.

After a few Sprints the velocity of a Scrum Team will most likely be predictable and would allow quite accurate estimation about the time needed until all entries in the Scrum Product Backlog will be completed. If the velocity of a Scrum Team is e.g. 30 story points and the total amount of remaining work is 155, we can predict that we need about 6 Sprint to complete all stories in the Backlog.

Supporting Concepts

CHAPTER TWENTY-SIX

USER STORY

What is a User Story?

In consultation with the customer or product owner, the team divides up the work to be done into functional increments called "user stories."

A user story is a tool used in Agile software development to capture a description of a software feature from an end-user perspective. A user story describes the type of user, what they want and why. A user story helps to create a simplified description of a requirement. User stories are often recorded on index cards, on Post-it notes, or in project management software. Depending on the project, user stories may be written by various stakeholders such as clients, users, managers or development team members.

Mike Cohn, a main contributor to the invention of Scrum software development methodology, says that "User stories are part of an agile approach that helps shift the focus from writing about requirements to talking about them. All agile user stories include a written sentence or two and, more importantly, a series of conversations about the desired functionality".

A user story is a lightweight method for quickly capturing the "who", "what" and "why" of a product requirement. In simple terms, user stories are stated ideas of requirements that express what users need. User stories are brief, with each element often containing fewer than 10 or 15 words each. User stories are "to-do" lists that help you determine the steps along the project's path. They help ensure that your process, as well as the resulting product, will meet your requirements.

A user story is defined incrementally, in three stages:

- The brief description of the need
- The conversations that happen during backlog grooming and iteration planning to solidify the details
- The tests that confirm the story's satisfactory completion

A good user story should be - INVEST:

- Independent: Should be self-contained in a way that allows to be released without depending on one another.
- Negotiable: Only capture the essence of user's need, leaving room for conversation. User story should not be written like contract.
- Valuable: Delivers value to end user.
- Estimable: User stories have to able to be estimated so it can be properly prioritized and fit into sprints.
- Small: A user story is a small chunk of work that allows it to be completed in about 3 to 4 days.
- Testable: A user story has to be confirmed via pre-written acceptance criteria.

How to Write User Stories?

User Story Template -
User stories only capture the essential elements of a requirement:

- Who it is for?
- What it expects from the system?
- Why it is important (optional?)?

One particular template, often referred to as "As a... I want to... So That..." is the most commonly recommended aids for teams and product owners starting to work with user stories and product backlog items in general:

As a (who wants to accomplish something)

I want to (what they want to accomplish)

So that (why they want to accomplish that thing)

An example:

As a bank customer

I want to withdraw money from an ATM

So that I'm not constrained by opening hours or lines at the teller's.

Lifecycle of a User story

Every user story is critically essential for the overall success of the product. The right strategy could be to implement one story per scrum. This way, you would be progressing towards clubbing the smaller pieces together that make the entire application work.

For a deeper insight, here is an overview of each of these user story life cycle stages.

1. To-Do - User Story Prioritization

Goal: Ranking user stories based on the urgency of solving the problem

Once the product owner has assembled the different types of user stories on the cards or post-its, the next task is to prioritize them. There might be tens or hundreds of stories, and the development team can't be acting on all of them at once; hence it's important to align them based on the urgency. This will be done at the time of Sprint Planning.

2. Monitoring Work Progress - Building Workflow Transparency

Goal: Building awareness around the progress of the user stories

The sprint backlog is already in place for all the user stories in the Agile Development process, in order of their preference.The status of the user story can be managed by the development team on a digital sprint taskboard. It will help maintain transparency by visualizing the flow and the progress of user stories. Moreover, it can also help estimate the gap between completed and pending user stories, which further helps in measuring team progress.

3. Quality Testing - To Check the Totality and Functionality of the User Story

Goal: To check the efficiency of the completed user story

The Agile development team might have done their bit with implementing the various ideas behind the user story. The quality team runs all sorts of quality tests such as unit testing, integration testing (with the flow of other user stories incorporated), functional testing, acceptance or beta testing, and so on.

In case of any bugs, the user story development process is iterated, to incorporate the changes. The team can again pick the tasks from the sprint backlog while the other user stories are put on hold.

4. User Acceptance Testing - To See Whether the User Story Appeals to the Users

Goal – Seeking validation from the end-users

The development team would have consulted a group of end-users when creating user stories for their expectations and pain points. Now, it is time to reach out to them again for the feedback on the feature built. This process is called user acceptance testing, and getting their approval indicates that the product is on the right track.

They may accept or reject it. In the latter case, remember that their opinion is everything, and user story lifecycle should be iterated until accepted by the users.

5. Story Completed - Getting on with MVP Development

Goal – To deliver a user story and move on to the next one

At this stage, the lifecycle of a user story ends. This means that the project manager has approved, the quality assurance team has given a go-ahead, and user testing has been a success. If the user stories accepted so far are enough to run the basic application, it's the ideal time to consider launching the MVP (Minimum Viable Product).

Now the project team can successfully and confidently move over to the next user story to continue with the overall project delivery lifecycle.

Points to Remember When Transitioning Across Stages

Here are some precautions and considerations that should be kept in mind by the entire product development team.

- Changes in user needs or market conditions can change the functional and business requirements at any time. The product teams should not hesitate from reworking on them.
- Split the user story structure if it seems too complicated to be implemented in one go.
- Proceed with another user story development only when the previous ones are accepted and completed.
- Use scrum in Agile Development as it offers a structured and disciplined way to complete tasks and deliver value.

- Conduct daily scrum meetings to keep track of the work in progress, along with fostering communication.
- Try not to misinterpret user stories, consult the end-users before coming to a conclusion.
- Instill product mindset over project mindset because one should hold the accountability of the product throughout its lifetime.

Benefits of a User story

Requirements always change as teams and customers learn more about the system as the project progresses. It's not exactly realistic to expect project teams to work off a static requirements list and then deliver functional software months later.

With user story approach, we replace big upfront design with a "just enough" approach. User stories reduce the time spent on writing exhaustive documentation by emphasizing customer-centric conversations. Consequently, user stories allow teams to deliver quality software more quickly, which is what customers prefer. There are quite a few benefits for adopting user story approach in agile development such as:

- The simple and consistent format saves time when capturing and prioritizing requirements while remaining versatile enough to be used on large and small features alike.
- Keep yourself expressing business value by delivering a product that the client really needs.
- Avoid introducing detail too early that would prevent design options and inappropriately lock developers into one solution.
- Avoid the appearance of false completeness and clarity.
- Get to small enough chunks that invite negotiation and movement in the backlog.
- Leave the technical functions to the architect, developers, testers, and so on.

CHAPTER TWENTY-SEVEN

ESTIMATION OF A USER STORY

A story point is a metric used in agile project management and development to estimate the difficulty of implementing a given user story, which is an abstract measure of effort required to implement it. In simple terms, a story point is a number that tells the team about the difficulty level of the story. Difficulty could be related to complexities, risks, and efforts involved.

Story point estimation, a kind of relative estimation, is typically performed at the Product Backlog Grooming Sessions and the Product Backlog is evaluated by the team who responsible for the actual development and testing work.

Story Points

When the development team conducts an estimation, it is recommended to abandon the traditional "human-day" assessment method, using the point of the story point, using the Fibonacci number (1, 2, 3, 5, 8, 13, 21...) to estimate the story point.

How to do Estimation of a User Story correctly?

Story points are a relative measurement unit, the first step your team should take is to define one story as the baseline, so that they can estimate the other stories comparing to that reference. According to the literature, the team should find the simplest story in the backlog, and assign 1 story point to it, after that, they use that story as baseline to estimate the other stories.

There are two types of scales used for creating estimation of user story point:

Linear scale (1,2,3,4,5,6,7...)

Fibonacci sequence numbers (0.5, 1, 2, 3, 5, 8, 13 ...)

It does not necessarily to be the smallest one, but the one that everyone within the team can resonate with. Once determined, sizing of all the user stories should be initiated by comparing them against the baseline.

When estimating new stories all you have to do is pick a story and say: "will this take longer than reference story x?" or "will it be less than reference y?" With enough reference stories there should be a suitable comparator to find a similar sized story and give it the same points or a bit more or a bit less based on a considered factor.

While estimating story points, we assign a point value to each story. Relative values are more important than the raw values. A story that is assigned 2 story points should be twice as much as a story that is assigned 1 story point. It should also be two-thirds of a story that is estimated 3 story points.By estimating in story points, the team reduces the dependency in individual developers; this is useful especially in dynamic teams where developers are often assigned to other projects after sprint delivery. For instance, if a user story is estimated as a 5 in effort (using Fibonacci sequence), it remains 5 regardless of how many developers are working on it

Story points define the effort in a time-box, so they do not change with time. For instance, in one hour an individual can walk, run, or climb, but the effort expended is clearly different. The gap progression between the terms in the Fibonacci sequence encourages the team to deliver carefully considered estimates. Estimates of 1, 2 or 3 imply similar efforts (1 being trivial), but if the team estimates an 8 or 13 (or higher), the impact on both delivery and budget can be significant. The value of using story points is that the team can reuse them by comparing similar work from previous sprints, but it should be recognized that estimates are relative to the team. For example, an estimate of 5 for one team could be a 2 for another having senior developers and higher skills.

In addition, it is important to note that when the single story point of the assessment is greater than 21, the user story needs to be split again, and the single user story point is no more than 8 is the most rational state.

Given below are few steps to reach the final decision of relative sizing:

- Analyze all user stories and identify the base or reference story. It is important for doing relative sizing. This story can be chosen from the current product backlog or the one, that we have done earlier. This story should be chosen as the reference story upon agreement of all members.
- Pick another story from the current Product Backlog and the team members are free to discuss any questions or doubts with the Product Owner, while understanding the requirements of the story. Product Owner is responsible for clarifying all their queries and doubts.
- Make a list of the things to be taken care while implementing the user story. These can be done by writing notes in the notes section of the tool or by adding bullet points on the story card. This is mostly done by the Scrum Master.

CHAPTER TWENTY-EIGHT

Velocity Of A Team

Velocity is an extremely simple, powerful method for accurately measuring the rate at which scrum development teams consistently deliver business value. It is an indication of the average amount of Product Backlog turned into an Increment of product during a Sprint by a Scrum Team, tracked by the Development Team for use within the Scrum Team. Thus, to calculate velocity of your agile team, simply add up the estimates of the features, user stories, requirements or backlog items successfully delivered in an iteration. It should the team:

- Predicting how much scope can be delivered by a specific date.
- Predicting a date for a fixed amount of scope to be delivered.
- Understanding our limits while defining the amount of scope we will commit for a sprint.

Velocity Chart - If a Scrum team has completed multiple sprints, the team can forecast release and product completion dates and plan future projects more accurately by reviewing the velocity report. Based on the velocity of previous sprints that the report illustrates, you can accomplish the following goals:

- Track how much effort your team has reported as complete for each sprint.
- Estimate how much backlog effort your team can handle in future sprints if your team composition and sprint duration stay constant.

How to calculate the Velocity of a Team?

There are some simple guidelines for estimating initial velocity of your Scrum team prior to completing the first few iterations, but after that point your team could use proven, historical measures of velocity estimation for sprint planning. Based on a series of past sprints, the estimation of velocity typically stabilizes and provides a more reliable basis for improving the accuracy of both short-term and longer-term planning of your Scrum projects.

Velocity is a measure of the amount of work a Team can tackle during a single Sprint and is the key metric in Scrum. Velocity is calculated at the end of the Sprint by summing up the Points for all fully completed User Stories. Points from partially-completed or incomplete stories should not be counted in calculating velocity.Knowing velocity, the team can compute (or revise) an estimate of how long the project will take to complete, based on the estimates associated with remaining user stories and assuming that velocity over the remaining iterations will remain approximately the same. This is generally an accurate prediction, even though rarely a precise one.

Step1 – Calculate the Velocity of the First iteration (Sprint)

At the end of each iteration, the team adds up effort estimates associated with user stories that were completed during that iteration. This total is called velocity.

An agile team has started work on an iteration, planning to complete stories A and B, estimated at 2 points each, and story C, estimated at 3 points. At the end of the iteration, stories A and B are 100% complete but C is only 80% complete. Agile teams generally acknowledge only two levels of completion, 0% done or 100% done. Therefore, C is not counted toward velocity, and velocity as of that iteration is 4 points.

Step 2 – Use the Velocity to estimate number of iteration needed

After knowing velocity in step 1, the team can compute (or revise) an estimate of how long the project will take to complete, based on the estimates associated with remaining user stories and assuming that velocity over the remaining iterations will remain approximately the same. This is generally an accurate prediction, even though rarely a precise one.

Suppose the user stories remaining represent a total of 40 points; the team's forecast of the remaining effort for the project is then 10 iterations.

Relationship of Velocity and Story Point in Scrum.

Story points are used to measure size and complexity which mean how long it takes us to finish it. Story point is a relative measure of the time it takes to complete a user story. It is a concept borrowed from XP. It is used to assess the difficulty of the story, not the promise of how long it will take. This is regardless of the size of the team or what is the task, you can use story points.

Relating Velocity to Story point:

- Teams often need to use "Velocity" as a measure of productivity to tell outsiders exactly how fast the Scrum team is.
- If the estimation of our story point is maintained throughout the project, it would make sense to use the story point to represent

"Velocity".

- If the consistency is not only in the team, but also in the cross team, even at the level of the entire company. This will not only measure productivity, but also compare the status of each team.
- If the value of the story point is stable, then it can be used as a reference for the release planning. You can evaluate the possible schedules afterwards.

How to Estimate Velocity More Accurately?

In Scrum, velocity help you to understand how long it will take your team to complete the product backlog. However, it typically takes few sprints for the team figure out a more stable velocity. To estimate more accurate velocity for your team, we can gain the experience based on the past track-record of the team. It will be more accurately forecasting of how many stories a Team can do in a Sprint. For forecasting purposes the average of the last three or four Sprint's Velocity should be used.

Suppose the new Scrum Team planned to complete 41 story points in their very first sprint. They eventually can only completed 38 story points, and rolled 6 story points over to the next sprint. So their velocity is 38.

The team should not add any partially-completed work towards the velocity. Only those user stories marked as 'Done' count, even if there's only a tiny bit of work left to do in the task.Based on just only one sprint, the velocity is not a very reliable metric for making predictions. (But it does give the team a sense of how much work they can commit to in a single sprint.) Let's track their progress for a few more sprints.

Now, the new team continuous the subsequently development from Sprint 1 – 4 and the story points in their first sprint is 38, 29 in their second, 38 in their third, and 39 in their fourth. So the estimation average of velocity after 4 sprints is 36.

This average, over just four sprints, is already much more useful than the snapshot we had after just one sprint. It's easy to imagine how, with a backlog of already-estimated user stories, we could use this velocity to make predictions. We could predict how quickly the team could get through all the work. And we could make educated guesses about what features we'd be able to deliver in upcoming releases.

CHAPTER TWENTY-NINE

COMMON MISTAKES IN SCRUM.

Agile project management holds a lot of promise for leaders. Those who have successfully made the switch in their organizations sing agile's praises, like the ability to rapidly course-correct, release software faster, and create happier teams and customers. But if you've been working at it for a while and you still aren't seeing the promised benefits, you might start to think that agile is more hype than substance, or that it isn't right for your organization.

The most common Scrum mistakes and How to avoid them:

Since the time I started my Scrum journey, I have witnessed a lot of teams moving to Scrum and trying to work around the framework. They try to crawl like a baby in the initial days and start walking along the path but I haven't come across any team adopting "SCRUM" as the way of working. At every corner, you can sense the non-scrum patterns and everyone putting the failure scenarios on the process or framework. It is really important to inspect the problem area and ways to move forward successfully.

I have put together a list of the common mistakes made while integrating Agile into routine work processes to provide you with an awareness to avoid them to get the best Agile environment for your projects to be successful.

1. The Daily stand-up meeting is not a status meeting

From the pre-scrum days, the team has been working in a mode where they are answerable either to their manager or the lead for their work. They are in the habit of working through the status meetings. However, Daily scrum or the stand-up meeting is far different, the daily stand-up is for the team as compared to an individual. I have noticed the daily scrum being directional, more of a status reporting to the lead or the Scrum Master.

Even in some cases, there will be an individual who will be taking notes from the meeting. This kind of daily scrum facilitation elevates the sense within the team of being micro-managed and being with someone focusing to keep track of what everyone is saying. This not only discourages the team, but it also dilutes the essence of doing the daily stand-up.

2. Expecting the Scrum Master to be the Project Manager

The most common mistake made in Agile is assuming that a Scrum Master is the same as a project manager or a lead developer. While none of these is correct, a scrum master is a role we haven't seen before. His role is to coach as well as facilitate his team and not manage the team. He provides guidance and advice to his team as well as the product owner on matters regarding the scrum framework.

By the nature of the work that Project Managers and Scrum Masters do, the two are not particularly closely aligned, even if it seems at first glance that they are. Managing a project is not the same as being a Scrum Master. Scrum Masters have the role of mentoring, teaching, coaching and facilitating, while the role of the Project Manager is to ensure that the project runs to time and budget. This means that the Scrum Master relies on more of the so-called "soft skills" involved with helping people to move forward, while the Project Manager takes a more methodical, and arguably more of a "hard skills" approach. While both roles have an interest in ensuring a high level of team performance and driving efficiency within the team, the ways in which they go about this are very different. The Scrum Master facilitates and coaches, while the Project Manager assesses risk and manages issues and conflicts.

3. Not raising obstacles early enough

One of the best things about Scrum is early addressal of impediments so that the team commitment is not hampered as Scrum is time-boxed. Most of the time, if the team member is blocked, they tend to wait or resolve on their own rather than raising a flag among the delivery team. It might work sometimes, but it is not an ideal approach. There may be cases where dependencies are involved.

Hence, raising the impediment upfront helps the teams and the team members adjust their workflow for minimal impact. The Scrum Master should maintain a log for impediments and track them to closure. The team should be provided with an environment to voice their issues without fear. Anything that is coming in their way of delivery should be raised immediately.

4. Incomplete user stories

"Often when teams sit down to complete estimates for the upcoming sprints, user stories are incomplete. This results in the inability to properly estimate, the likelihood of scope creep, and an inability to deliver what was originally planned for the sprint. Incomplete requirements require lengthy back and forth between the engineering and product teams, thus slowing down the delivery process. Prior to estimating sessions and committing work to a sprint, having complete requirements is essential." - Holly Knoll, business coach and creator of The Consultant Code

5. An Un-Ready Product Backlog

A product backlog that isn't "ready" is one of the most common reasons for sprint failure and for unmotivated teams. It is also a root cause for low delivery velocity and not delivering high value. Most new Product Owners aren't ready to be productive on their own. They need instruction, coaching, and hand-holding for the first few sprints as they learn to develop and maintain a product backlog that has enough valuable features estimated at a high level, and prioritized by business value. Preparing the backlog well ahead of the next sprint(s) is a must. You never want the team to run out of work to do, and that work must be of highest value at that point in time as prioritized by the Product Owner. Being a Product Owner can be time-consuming. Set the right expectations, provide all the training, and help the Product Owner to keep the flow of value coming.

6. Not Conducting Retrospective Meetings After Every Sprint

A retrospective generally, is a look back at events that took place, or works that were produced, in the past. One of the twelve principles behind the Agile Manifesto is "At regular intervals, the team reflects on how to become more effective, then tunes and adjusts its behavior accordingly". Unfortunately the Sprint Retrospective is often treated like an add-on or a luxury, and performed only "if there's time". The fact is, Agile is all about adjustments here and there, fine tuning and responding to change. It's really hard to adjust and fine tune if we don't pause to find out where adjustments are needed.

7. Processes and Tools Over Individuals and Interactions (mindset)

Nowadays, we have effective and efficient online tools to handle the backlog and the workflow, and the same goes for communication too. With such a vast variety of tools, the teams tend to rely more on them rather than individual interactions. I was surprised to see a development team member dropping an email for the issues in the code after testing, this is not what we want, right? We need to understand the background and why do they prefer written communication over face to face interactions. Are there any trust issues?

The Scrum Master can set some working agreements with the delivery team to overcome such issues. The team will be defining how they want to work, and they would be setting their own rules. The focus should be more on collaboration and interactions rather than process or tool, but that doesn't mean they can go away with it, it is still important!

8. Do we need a Scrum Master?

As prescribed by Agile and Scrum Guide, the delivery team consists of a Product Owner, development team, and the Scrum Master. Each role has its own responsibilities and their own boundaries. This gets thinned when the role of a Scrum Master is not taken seriously. In some of the teams, I have observed, the team members play a dual role, for example, product owner plus a Scrum Master or Scrum Master plus developer.

It is really critical to understand that if someone with another role plays a Scrum Master, then they are hindering the person's ability to focus on helping the teams, following processes or removing impediments. It is a very crucial role which helps the ship to sail through along with shielding the team from outer distractions.

9. Resistance to culture change

"The greatest challenge or roadblock for the data team is culture. For too long, the data teams have not had to consult with others. They viewed themselves and were treated by management as insular, not subject to the demands of the enterprise. This is no longer the case. Changing the culture around data service teams will be the biggest challenge. Feedback loops and blameless postmortems would benefit the data services teams, but they are very different from how they do their jobs today.

"One of the hallmarks of agile is focusing more on the process and less on the tools. That's a difficult idea for database professionals. Moreover, flexibility and nimbleness are not exactly words one would use to describe most database teams. But that needs to change now. When other parts of the organization adopt agile, it puts an immense amount of pressure on database teams.

10. Commitment based on assumptions

Another common mistake that I have noticed is around making the commitment for a sprint based on assumptions. Why? Because the team is hesitant to ask back, as per the Agile framework, there was no proper grooming done to make it free of assumptions. Most of the times, teams are asked to commit just because the requirement is on priority. They are not given enough time to think through or brainstorm, they just commit. This not only leads to carryover but also lowers the morale of the team.

It is important to clarify the queries with the product owner, talk about the dependencies and constraints. Continuous communication should prevail between the product owner and the development team throughout the sprint. Scrum now encourages the Development Team to forecast which Product Backlog Items it will deliver by the end of the Sprint.

11. No outputs from the retrospectives

Retrospectives are considered the most important ceremony is Scrum because that is the time when the team inspects themselves and thinks through the actions to make it better next time. There can be several ways of conducting the retrospectives, but the most important part is the tracking of action items discussed in the meeting. If the action items are not closed, the trust on the ceremony gets impacted, the team will start taking it as no value add to the time being spent.

Hence, it is the responsibility of the delivery team to make sure the items discussed should get closed, here, the Scrum Master can help with the facilitation and tracking. Every retrospective should include the status on the last retro items. This gives the confidence to the team that they are being heard and they feel empowered too.

12. Inapt physical environment

Ideally, the Scrum team should be sitting together, all the development team member, Scrum Master, and the product owner should be in a single room or in a single bay. Focus is more on the individual and interactions and face-to-face communication, there are cases where the teams are not collocated. In my last project, there was a team, where the product owner was on the south side of the globe and the delivery team on the west.

And the story is not ending here, and even the team members were divided into two different locations in the west. Ahhh! It gets difficult to work with this big distributed team. It not only impacts the collaborative efforts, but it also hampers productivity. Hence, there should be efforts to help the team move together.

13. Missing DoR and DoD

As mentioned in point number 5, the existence of Definition of Ready (DoR) is important to ensure the team is committing the right work. The definition of ready has few parameters as set by the team, to say, when they are good to commit stories in a sprint. In the same way, the team should have Definition of Done, to say when the item committed in a sprint is 'Done'.

Both DoR and DoD enhances the quality of the product being delivered. The Scrum Master should ensure the creation of this agreement happens before the start of the sprint and it gets revisited once in every three months or whatever frequency they are comfortable in. If the team has defined their DoR and DoD, the dependencies, risks, and unknowns are minimized.

14. Is it a team or a horde?

It is always easy to work with smaller groups, even the Scrum guide talks about having a team size of seven to nine members. When you are working with a large Scrum team, communication becomes the biggest challenge. As the size is big, the ceremonies too will take a long time and with shorter sprints, these meetings become a pain for the team. If you have 3 people then you have 6 communication points. Everyone communicates with 2 others. If you have 5 team members then it's 20. For 9 member team, it's 72.

This is a lot of communication and interaction points in a team. Even the information might get lost in the web of combinations created within the team.

15. Thinking Agile means no documentation

In every boot camps or training, I get this question asked: "Is Agile about NO documentation?" We, in Agile, do documentation but the focus is on 'Comprehensive Documentation'. Even one of the points from manifesto talks about 'Working Software over Comprehensive Documentation'.

Nowhere in Agile principles or Manifesto, we say NO to documentation. It doesn't mean that you should not create documentation; it means you should create documentation that delivers value and at the same time does not obstruct the team's progress.

CHAPTER THIRTY

TESTING IN AGILE

Agile methodologies for software development have been included in improving the testing methods for products as well. This software testing process is known as Agile Testing Methodology. It works with the iterative approach to software development that comes with the Agile methodology, in the sense that it focuses on the gradually developing requirements of any product from the customer and testing team. The development process with each iteration is then aligned to these requirements.

Normally, the testing methods are sequential, but when it comes to Agile testing, the process is continuous. The Agile Testing Methodology process begins at the start of the project itself and it is integrated with the development team. The developers and testers both have a common objective that they work together to achieve delivering a product of high quality.

Another evolution in agile testing is that testers are no longer a separate organizational unit. Testers are now part of the agile development team. In many cases, agile organizations don't have dedicated "testers" or "QA engineers"; instead, everyone on the team is responsible for testing. Agile testing is a testing practice that follows the rules and principles of agile software development.

The agile manifesto, has several points that are especially relevant for testers:

Agile Manifesto Directive	Implication for Testing
Individuals and interactions over processes and tools	Testers should work closely with developers, product owners, and customers to understand what is being developed, who it is for, and what will make it successful.
Working software over comprehensive documentation	Testers in the agile world do not have a book of requirements they can test against. They need to carefully define and refine acceptance criteria together with their teams and test against those criteria.
Responding to change over following a plan	Agile testers must prioritize and re-prioritize their tests, focusing on what will help the team reach its goal, minimize risk and keep customers happy.
Collaborating with customers over contract negotiation	Whether they have direct contact with customers or not, testers in an agile environment should be focused on what matters for the customer – which can vary from product to product. Customers may focus on new features, stability, security or other requirements, depending on their needs and the product's maturity.

Agile testing refers to a software testing practice that follows different principles of agile software development. In other words, agile testing means testing software for defects or any other issues quickly or within the context of agile and give quick feedback for better and faster development of the project.

As companies grow, agile testing teams often rely on software testing tools to solve challenges that can ultimately speed-up the release of feedback making sure. Most teams look for collaboration features, automated or customized reporting and finding ways to avoid repeated efforts. Choosing the right tool will depend on the requirements of each team. Pairing up with other Agile Lifecycle Development Tools, Agile testing tools can deliver effective results by coexisting in integrated environments. Such is the case for Atlassian Marketplace and Microsoft Visual Studio.

Some test management tools support Agile testing by getting teams involved earlier in the SDLC to continuously build test scenarios as stories evolve.Teams often look for a solution that can deliver a combination of automated and manual testing.

Life Cycle of Agile Testing

The Agile Testing Methodology can be divided into five main phases. This life cycle takes place from the beginning of the project until it is complete. The phases are as follows:

1. Impact Assessment – This is the first phase where testers gather inputs from all the stakeholders and users and given to the development team as feedback for their next iteration.
2. Agile Testing Planning – The second phase of Agile testing involves bringing together the stakeholders to plan all the details of the testing process such as the schedule, frequency of the meetings, and the deliverables needed.
3. Release Readiness – The third phase of the testing process includes reviewing all the features that the development team has deployed in the product and checking them for bugs.
4. Daily Scrums – This phase is not necessarily the fourth phase, but is actually the daily meetings for the team to check the status of the project on a regular basis.
5. Test Agility Review – The final phase is the Test Agility Review phase, where the tea meets with the stakeholders to review

all the features deployed in the iteration and assess the overall project.

Agile Test Plan

Agile test plan includes types of testing done in that iteration like test data requirements, infrastructure, test environments, and test results. Unlike the waterfall model, in an agile model, a test plan is written and updated for every release. Typical test plans in agile includes:

- Testing Scope
- New functionalities which are being tested
- Level or Types of testing based on the features complexity
- Load and Performance Testing
- Infrastructure Consideration
- Mitigation or Risks Plan
- Resourcing
- Deliverables and Milestones

Agile Testing Strategies

Agile testing life cycle spans through four stages:

1. Iteration 0

During the first stage or iteration 0, you perform initial setup tasks. It includes identifying people for testing, installing testing tools, scheduling resources (usability testing lab), etc. The following steps are set to achieve in Iteration 0 :

- Establishing a business case for the project
- Establish the boundary conditions and the project scope

- Outline the key requirements and use cases that will drive the design trade-offs
- Outline one or more candidate architectures
- Identifying the risk
- Cost estimation and prepare a preliminary project

2. Construction Iterations

The second phase of agile testing methodology is Construction Iterations, the majority of the testing occurs during this phase. This phase is observed as a set of iterations to build an increment of the solution. In order to do that, within each iteration, the team implements a hybrid of practices from XP, Scrum, Agile modeling, and agile data and so on.

In construction iteration, the agile team follows the prioritized requirement practice: With each iteration, they take the most essential requirements remaining from the work item stack and implement them.

Construction iteration is classified into two, confirmatory testing and investigative testing. Confirmatory testing concentrates on verifying that the system fulfills the intent of the stakeholders as described to the team to date, and is performed by the team. While the investigative testing detects the problem that confirmatory team has skipped or ignored. In Investigative testing, tester determines the potential problems in the form of defect stories. Investigative testing deals with common issues like integration testing, load/ stress testing, and security testing.

Again for, confirmatory testing there are two aspects developer testing and agile acceptance testing. Both of them are automated to enable continuous regression testing throughout the lifecycle. Confirmatory testing is the agile equivalent of testing to the specification.

Agile acceptance testing is a combination of traditional functional testing and traditional acceptance testing as the development team, and stakeholders are doing it together. While developer testing is a mix of traditional unit testing and traditional service integration testing. Developer testing verifies both the application code and the database schema.

3. Release End Game Or Transition Phase

The goal of "Release, End Game" is to deploy your system successfully into production. The activities include in this phase are training of end users, support people and operational people. Also, it includes marketing of the product release, back-up & restoration, finalization of system and user documentation.

The final agile methodology testing stage includes full system testing and acceptance testing. In accordance to finish your final testing stage without any obstacles, you should have to test the product more rigorously while it is in construction iterations. During the end game, testers will be working on its defect stories.

4. Production

After the release stage, the product will move to the production stage.

The Agile Testing Quadrants

The agile testing quadrants separate the whole process in four Quadrants and help to understand how agile testing is performed.

Quadrant I– The internal code quality is the main focus in this quadrant, and it consists of test cases which are technology driven and are implemented to support the team, it includes :

- Unit Tests
- Component Tests

Quadrant II– It contains test cases that are business driven and are implemented to support the team. This Quadrant focuses on the requirements. The kind of test performed in this phase is :

- Testing of examples of possible scenarios and workflows
- Testing of User experience such as prototypes
- Pair testing

Quadrant III – This quadrant provides feedback to quadrants one and two. The test cases can be used as the basis to perform automation testing. In this quadrant, many rounds of iteration reviews are carried out which builds confidence in the product. The kind of testing done in this quadrant is :

- Usability Testing
- Exploratory Testing
- Pair testing with customers
- Collaborative testing
- User acceptance testing

Quadrant IV– This quadrant concentrates on the non-functional requirements such as performance, security, stability, etc. With the help of this quadrant, the application is made to deliver the non-functional qualities and expected value.

- Non-functional tests such as stress and performance testing
- Security testing with respect to authentication and hacking
- Infrastructure testing
- Data migration testing
- Scalability testing

Agile methodology in software testing involves testing as early as possible in the software development lifecycle. It demands high customer involvement and testing code as soon as it becomes available. The code should be stable enough to take it to system testing. Extensive regression testing can be done to make sure that the bugs are fixed and tested. Mainly, Communication between the teams makes agile model testing success.

Principles of Agile Testing.

There are different principles that are involved when teams want to practice Agile Testing Methodology to help them achieve their goals. These include:

- All Agile Testing is continuous: Agile teams make testing a regular practice and perform tests regularly so that they can guarantee the continuous progress of the overall project and product development.
- The feedback in Agile testing is continuous: Due to the regular nature of Agile testing, the feedback provided to the developers and stakeholders is also continuous and takes place on an ongoing basis to make sure all business needs of the product are being met.
- Agile testing includes the entire Agile team: Unlike the traditional method of testing where only the test team is responsible for the testing in the software development life cycle, Agile testing involves the developers, the testers as well as the business analysts to test the product.
- Agile testing reduces the time of feedback response: Agile testing involves the entire team as well as stakeholders with each iteration of the project, giving the team continuous feedback throughout the project's lifecycle, which reduces the time to include the response to the feedback given.
- Agile testing focuses on creating simplified and clean code: All the defects found by the Agile team are fixed in the same iteration, which means the code used by the developers is both clean and simplified.

- Agile testing reduces documentation: Instead of creating a new checklist, Agile teams reuse their checklist made by the team and just add to it while testing instead of focusing on the incidental details.
- Agile projects are always test-driven: With Agile teams, the product is tested when it is being implemented instead of after the implementation process.

Agile Testing Methods

There are four main methods of Agile testing discussed in detail below:

1. Behaviour Driven Development (BDD)

BDD encourages communication between project stakeholders so all members understand each feature, prior to the development process. In BDD, testers, developers, and business analysts create "scenarios", which facilitate example-focused communication. Scenarios are written in a specific format, the Gherkin Given/When/Then syntax. They contain information on how a feature behaves in different situations with varying input parameters. These are known as "executable specifications" as they are made up of both specifications and inputs to the automated tests.

The idea of BDD is that the team creates scenarios, builds tests around those scenarios which initially fail, and then builds the software functionality that makes the scenarios pass. It is different from traditional Test-Driven Development (TDD) in that complete software functionality is tested, not just individual components.

Best practices for testers using a BDD methodology:

- Streamline documentation to ensure the process is efficient.

- Embrace a "three amigos" approach, where the developer, product owner, and tester work together to define scenarios and tests.
- Use a declarative test framework, such as Cucumber, to specify criteria.
- Build automated tests and reuse them across scenarios.
- Have business analysts write test cases and learn the Gherkin syntax.

2. Acceptance Test-Driven Development (ATDD)

In the ATDD method of Agile testing, team members with different perspectives are involved. These members include the following:

- Customers
- Developers
- Testers

They meet to create acceptance tests which include the perspectives of the parties mentioned above and aim to include the different points of focus for each party.

- Customers are focused on finding the problems that need to be solved.
- The developers are focused on finding the ways in which the customers' problems can be solved.
- The testers are focused on finding problem areas.

This method of testing represents the user's point of view. They focus on the 'how' aspect of the features and help in checking if each feature works the way it was intended to.

Best practices for testers using an ATDD methodology include:

- Interact directly with customers to align expectations, for example, through focus groups.
- Involve customer-facing team members to understand customer needs, including. customer service agents, sales representatives, and account managers.
- Develop acceptance criteria according to customer expectations.
- Prioritize two questions: How should we validate that the system performs a certain function? Will customers want to use the system when it has this function?

3. Exploratory Testing

The Exploratory testing method focuses on creating workable software over documentation of the process. The design and execution phase of these tests go hand in hand. The main priority of this testing method is customer collaboration and interactions over contract negotiation and processes and tools.

This method of testing is the most adaptable to any changes because the testers explore the application to identify its functionalities. They learn and understand the application so that they can design and execute their tests based on what they find. It is a customized approach to testing.

Best practices for exploratory testing:

- Organize functionality in the application, using a spreadsheet, mind map etc.
- Even though there is no detailed documentation of how tests were conducted, track which software areas were or were not covered with exploratory testing.
- Focus on areas and scenarios in the software which are at high risk or have high value for users.

- Ensure testers document their results so they can be accountable for areas of software they tested.

4. Session-Based Testing

This method is similar to exploratory testing, but is more orderly, aiming to ensure the software is tested comprehensively. It adds test charters, which helps testers know what to test, and test reports which allow testers to document what they discover during a test. Tests are conducted during time-boxed sessions.

Each session ends with a face-to-face brief between tester(s) and either the developers responsible, scrum master or manager, covering the five PROOF points:

- What was done in the test (Past).
- What the tester discovered or achieved (Results).
- Any problems that got in the way (Obstacles).
- Remaining areas to be tested (Outlook).
- How the tester feels about the areas of the product they tested (Feelings).

Best practices for session-based testing include:

- Define a goal so testers are clear about priorities of testing in the current sprint.
- Develop a charter that states areas of the software to test, when the session will occur and for how long, which testers will conduct the session, etc.
- Run uninterrupted testing sessions with a fixed, predefined length.
- Document activities, notes, and also takeaways from the face-to-face brief in a session report.

CHAPTER THIRTY-ONE

HOW CAN WE ADOPT AGILE FOR A NEW TEAM?

An Agile adoption effort may be divided into three phases: Readiness, Deployment, and Support. Throughout each phase, it is very beneficial to on-board an Agile Coach to improve your chances of success. The Agile Coach helps a team adopt and improve Agile methods and practice. They should have years of Agile experience having implemented Agile on several product teams and have participated as a ScrumMaster, Product Owner, or Agile team member on an Agile project. Their hands-on and consulting experience helps the team stay focused on the tasks in the journey to Agile. Let's examine the tasks within each phase more thoroughly.

Agile Readiness

The goal of the readiness phase of Agile adoption is to understand the current state of the product team, setting the expectation for change, and to establish an overall strategy and plan for the engagement. This phase typically lasts about one to three months.

Tasks to consider getting the product team ready include:

- Determine suitability of product - While some may state that Agile methods can be applied to all product development, some products have more uncertainty than others and are more likely to benefit more from applying Agile methods and practices. This analysis can help you target the product teams that can benefit most from Agile, so that you get the biggest benefit for the effort.
- Determine willingness of team - This involves evaluating the team for their willingness to move to Agile. It is important to understand those teams and team members that are Agile friendly, those that are unfriendly to Agile, and those that are uncertain about the changes it will bring. This analysis allows you to respond accordingly by either improving team member willingness or adjusting the team composition.
- Determine capability of team - This involves evaluating the team's capability in applying Agile. It is important to determine what skill sets you have on the team and the team understanding of implementing Agile. This allows you to determine the type and level of Agile and engineering training that is needed by team members.
- Assess engineering practices and Agile mindset of the team - This is to determine what engineering practices are being applied and how effective they are. This also assesses how Agile the team may already be in the approach they use to software development. This is applicable to existing product teams who have a release already under their belt. This allows you know which engineering practices are team strengths and which need improvement.
- Identify an Agile Coach - Your coach should be an Agile professional experienced in applying and executing Agile methods and practices on product teams, with the capability of completing the tasks included in the readiness phase. An experienced Agile Coach will increase the chances of a

successful Agile adoption.

- Establish a strategy and plan for implementing Agile - Much like a backlog and Sprint Planning, this is where you establish a prioritized list of tasks and implement them within a sprint context . Consider using the tasks in this article as a starting point. This should be initiated by discussing the goals of the Agile adoption effort with the team to ensure their understanding. This will help make certain that the work is planned and prioritized effectively.

- Establish periodic progress meetings - Much like like the Daily Stand-up, this is where the team or at least a core group meet regularly to assess the progress of the prioritized tasks. This ensures that there is a focus on an effective adoption of Agile.

- Establish Agile Roles - This is where we structure the team into appropriate Agile roles (e.g., Agile team member, ScrumMaster, and Product Owner) and determine if more than one Scrum team is needed (e.g., multiple Scrum teams that make up a large project team). This may require some restructuring to reduce functional relationships to improve team empowerment. The purpose is to ensure that we have a organizational structure that is most suited to Agile.

- Determine Stakeholder support - This involves identifying which stakeholders (e.g., Senior Management) are the Agile sponsors, then determining how supportive and Agile friendly they are. Identifying their level of support allows you to be aware of friend or foe, potentially increase the level of Agile knowledge and support of the stakeholder and be aware of any risks to Agile support.

- Establish the Agile methodology and practices framework - This involves building a set of Agile practices (e.g., Sprint Planning, Story Writing, Daily Stand-up, End of Sprint Review, Retrospective, Scrum of Scrums, Continuous Integration and Build, etc.), techniques (e.g., sizing, etc.), and criteria (e.g., "done", acceptance, etc.) for the product team. This also includes establishing an Agile framework that works within the governance context of the organization. The result is that the team will have an Agile structure to begin with and can hone practices and process over time. This can also be used as the basis of Agile team training.

- Consider Agile tool needs - This involves determining if Agile tools will be part of the initial Agile deployment, and what tools may be used to help you get started. An Agile tool evaluation is typically in order unless there are already defined Agile tool standards within your company. Agile tools are commonly thought of as Agile planning tools, but may also include test tools, continuous integration tools, and collaboration tools (amongst others). The benefit with tooling is that it may help support the Agile process, improve interaction with distributed teams, and enable automation. If the team is fortunate enough to be collocated, then a physical team wall is a suitable replacement for an Agile planning tool.

- Focus on Agile mindset and cultural shift - While it is important to provide a focus on Agile practices and tools, a specific focus on establishing an Agile mindset is important. This involves a focus on self-empowerment, servant-leader, assertiveness, volunteering, etc. The benefit is that this ensures there is a focus on the Agile mindset.

Agile Deployment

The goal of the deployment phase is to execute the Agile approach and practices and help the team apply them to the project. This phase typically lasts about one to three months. Tasks to consider getting Agile deployed within product teams include:

1. Set up the Agile Planning tool - During the readiness phase, there should have been a focus on Agile tool needs, and if so, a selection of a tool or tools. Once the tool has been selected, approved, ordered, and received, it is time to install and deploy

the tool for team use. This ensures that the team has a common interface, and access to the user stories and work ahead.

2. Provide Agile Training - This involves providing role-specific training to those that will be applying Agile. While off-the-shelf Agile training is fine, it is beneficial to incorporate context-specific details into the training or provide a one-off training that walks the team through the Agile methodology and practices framework that was established during the readiness phase. Types of training to consider are:

- Agile for the Team – Agile training with a view from the team's perspective. This should include the Agile methodology and practices with a specific focus on Agile engineering practices
- Product Owner training – Agile training with a view from the Product Owner's perspective. Specific focus should be given to writing user stories.
- ScrumMaster training - Typically Certified ScrumMaster (CSM) training. Given the abundance of CSM training held throughout the world, it may be best to approach this using an external vendor.
- Agile Tool training - If there is an Agile planning tool, it is beneficial to train the Product Owner (to establish and manage their backlog), the Agile team (to refine stories and use their wall), and the ScrumMaster (to manage burndowns and other reporting).

While there is an obvious benefit to Agile training, it is important to ensure there is an emphasis on adapting to the Agile mindset.

- Deploy the Agile methodology and Agile practices - As the project gets kicked off, and Agile methods and practices start getting used, this where the Agile Coach (or someone experienced in Agile) helps deploys the Agile practices to aid in improving the execution. This may involve helping apply the practices for the first three sprints and providing coaching and mentoring to the team to correctly apply the practices. This ensures that the Agile practices are being understood, deployed as defined, and applied with an Agile mindset.

- Periodic Meetings to ensure deployment is on track and directionally correct - As the deployment phase is underway, it is important to have brief periodic meetings to ensure there is a focus on the deployment activities. The benefit of doing this is to ensure the team sees that Agile adoption is not seen as a trivial effort, but does have the focus on the leaders on the team.

Agile Support

The goal of this phase is to provide the necessary support (e.g., coaching and mentoring) to the team deploying Agile, and the validation to ensure that practices have been implemented and improved as appropriate. This phase typically lasts about six to nine months. By the end of the Agile Support phase, internal Agile Champions should emerge, and the team should be able to operate effectively without the Agile Coach. Tasks to consider during the Agile support phase include:

- Provide continued Coaching and Mentoring - This involves continued interaction with the team to resolve issues and challenges seen within the project context. This ensures the team knows that you are available to answer questions and assist as needed. It is not uncommon for some folks to want to regress back to a more waterfall or hierarchical approach, so it is particularly valuable to have the Agile Coach remain available to redirect the approach back to Agile.
- Provide In-session Validation of Practices - This involves occasionally attending Agile related sessions (e.g., Sprint Planning, Daily Stand-ups, End of Sprint Reviews, etc.) to validate the application of the Agile practices within the team.

This helps the team understand if they are applying Agile appropriately and can help them hone (e.g., inspect and adapt) as appropriate.

- Provide periodic check-in meetings to monitor direction - These are short periodic sessions where the progress of the Agile adoption is discussed. This gets less frequent over time. Agile adoption is a cultural shift which takes time, so these sessions ensure there is still focus on the implementation, and risks and issues continue to be discussed and resolved.

- Provide periodic Agile assessments to gauge adoption level - This is where you assess the current state of the software engineering practices being applied as well as the Agile mindset of the team. This provides the team with a new baseline of adoption which can be compared to previous Agile adoption assessments. This allows you to gauge the level of adoption that has occurred and to determine where to target improvements.

- Provide additional focus on tools and automation - This is where you ascertain if additional tools or automation could help the team. Sometimes when velocity plateaus, this can be the result of a lack of automation. While tools should not be the primary focus of an Agile implementation, tooling and automation can help the team incorporate effective QA and Configuration Management (CM) practices (amongst others) and improve team velocity.

- Groom local Agile Champions - This is where you continue to work with the Agile ScrumMaster(s), Agile Team, Product Owner(s) to ensure they have the true Agile mindset and are applying Agile effectively. This is where you would identify a person or two who is passionate about Agile and has the experience to help others apply it effectively. The benefit is that once the Agile Coach departs, there is a local Agile Champion that has been groomed to take over and keep the team focused on the Agile approach.

Scrum Or Not To Scrum?

Scrum is a project management technique that helps teams build large or complicated products. It encourages collaboration and improvement by encouraging the team to self-organize, learn by doing, and reflect on their successes and failures.

In a nutshell, Scrum helps teams break down the larger project into smaller, more manageable pieces called sprints. During a sprint, the team focuses on that one part, and nothing else. By working on that smaller part of the larger project, teams have the flexibility to change and adapt their approach, improving the project as it progresses.

With frequent check-ins, Scrum keeps the entire process transparent and helps team members incorporate changes as they receive feedback about the project. It also allows the team to work on small areas of the project when other areas are "stuck" and the problems are being resolved.

Who Uses Scrum

Everyone! There are no rules about what industries or which teams can use Scrum or Agile. Any team that could benefit from a collaborative process or ongoing feedback can use Scrum.

However, Scrum is most often found on software development and engineering teams. This is mainly because these industries tend to create products that need regular and frequent updates.

For example, app developers don't create their app, release it, and never update it . They look at customer reviews, learn from that feedback, and tweak the app to make it better. Then, they look at the feedback on the update, learn from the new feedback, and tweak the app again. And again. And again.

The updates don't only happen in response to user feedback, though. As the operating system changes, the app developers update their apps to work with the new system. That requires them to collaborate with the operating system programmers to make sure the app can run on the new system. And, as often happens, when one side finds a bug, they report it to the other side in an effort to help improve one another's products.

Pros:

1. Scrum is a framework that can help you manage your project more effectively and make better use of time and budget.
2. Scrum is a guarantee of transparency of all stages of the project.
3. It is estimated that Scrum is currently the most effective method of managing IT projects.
4. One of the principles of Scrum is to focus on minimizing errors. Thanks to this approach (for example, running numerous tests) you can be sure that the project is maintained at the highest quality level.
5. The implementation of the project using Scrum is divided into so-called sprints. During their lifetime, the team focuses on the development of strictly defined functionalities. Sprints are a great way to achieve progressive and sustainable product development.
6. Scrum is a very flexible methodology. If the customer wants to make any changes or extend the product with new functionalities, usually there are no problems with that. This kind of elasticity is ensured by sprints.
7. Scrum provides task prioritization. First, you develop the ticks of the main "to do", and then you also implement a "backlog task" list. This last one includes tasks that can be described as "nice to have". In this way, you can be sure that the team is currently working on the most important functionalities.
8. Scrum is also an effective methodology from the client's perspective. Thanks to daily meetings, the client can be up to date with all current work. His feedback is also taken into account.

9. Daily meetings help to identify emerging threats and problems that can be quickly solved.
10. The Scrum methodology is affordable for the budget. You can regularly control and estimate all expenses.

Cons:

1. The success of your project may be at risk if a team member is not involved or does his job slower than the others.
2. The Scrum Master role is critical. If he does not perform his duties duly, it may lead to delays in the project.
3. Scrum is ideal for 3-9-person teams. In the case of larger teams, there may be problems in management efficiency.
4. Daily meetings can be frustrating for team members who present the results of their work.
5. The unexpected departure of one team member may harm the progress of the entire project.
6. The date of product delivery and the sprint time limit shall not apply to Scrum.

Go with Scrum or not?

Scrum is not an ideal methodology for all kinds of projects, but I still recommend you use it. Especially when you are responsible for IT projects. If you plan all the work thoroughly, you have a greater chance to achieve high efficiency and be successful.

Consider all the pros and cons that I have mentioned here and think about whether your project meets the criteria that will allow the effective development of the project using Scrum. If you correctly identify your needs and possible threats, I am convinced that Scrum will help you achieve success.

Conclusion

Agile was born to simplify the lives of software developers, testers, and the organizations.

If learning an Agile method and implementing it are demanding you to be Einstein, it signals that you need to be flexible and shift your creativity-discipline equilibrium more towards the creative side of Agile development.Your transition from plan based approach to Agile should result in the reduction of management overhead and lessen the burden of formalities from your creative development team.

Agile and lean approach exist to help solving problems. Many teams encounter similar problems:

- Key requirements change
- The agreements signed at the beginning of project are insufficient for the problems the team encountering now
- The team can't release anything at the desired release date. Everything is partially done and nothing is fully done

Agile is a culture change, NOT just a different life cycle.Agile approach create a culture of working with transparency, driven by value, collaborating across organization, enable a team to deliver value often.

Agile methods and processes forms a basic tool of instrument towards the developmentof any software and the realization of its success as it benefits the teams, project owners and stakeholders. The agile method and process as a means of software development provides different iterations which form the basis for exchange of ideas and the making of appropriate changes that in the long run will fit the customers' needs enhancing the cultivation of asuccessful project, this ensures minimal drawbacks related to software development since it develops high standard requirement on the team members since it can be incorporated on their existing body of knowledge.

Agile values are beneficial to the project development process and promote communication both horizontally and vertically throughout the organization. Agile enhances innovation through high-performance multidisciplinary teams and ensures business value by direct client involvement throughout the entire delivery process.Enhanced communication, teamwork, collaboration, and organizational change improve the adoption of higher business value products during the preliminary stages and throughout the project lifecycle.

Ensuring governance and enterprise suitability
are a challenge ...